Y0-ABA-357

THE ABUNDANT LIFE
BIBLE
AMPLIFIER

HEBREWS

WILLIAM G. JOHNSSON, Ph.D.

THE ABUNDANT LIFE
BIBLE
AMPLIFIER

HEBREWS

**Full Assurance for
Christians Today**

GEORGE R. KNIGHT
General Editor

Pacific Press Publishing Association
Boise, Idaho
Oshawa, Ontario, Canada

Edited by Marvin Moore
Designed by Tim Larson
Typeset in 11/14 Janson Text

Library of Congress Cataloging-in-Publication Data:

Johnsson, William G., 1934-
    Hebrews: full assurance for Christians today / by William
G. Johnsson.
      p.   cm. — (A Bible amplifier book)
    ISBN 0-8163-1201-X. — ISBN 0-8163-1200-1 (pbk.)
    1. Bible. N. T. Hebrews—Criticism, interpretation, etc.
2. Seventh-day Adventists—Doctrines. 3. Adventists—Doctrines. 4. Sabbatarians—Doctrines. I. Title. II. Series.
BS2775.2.J62   1994
227'.8706—dc20   93-36095
                                             CIP

94 95 96 97 98 • 5 4 3 2

CONTENTS

DEDICATION

To my father, Joel Johnsson,
who knew the Book more than anyone I ever met;
who knew the Man of the Book;
and who introduced both to me.

The Abundant Life Bible Amplifier series is aimed at helping readers understand the Bible better. Rather than merely offering comments on or about the Bible, each volume seeks to enable people to study their Bibles with fuller understanding.

To accomplish that task, scholars who are also proven communicators have been selected to author each volume. The basic idea underlying this combination is that scholarship and the ability to communicate on a popular level are compatible skills.

While the Bible Amplifier is written with the needs and abilities of laypeople in mind, it will also prove helpful to pastors and teachers. Beyond individual readers, the series will be useful in church study groups and as guides to enrich participation in the weekly prayer meeting.

Rather than focusing on the details of each verse, the Bible Amplifier series seeks to give readers an understanding of the themes and patterns of each biblical book as a whole and how each passage fits into that context. As a result, the series does not seek to solve all the problems or answer all the questions that may be related to a given text. In the process of accomplishing the goal for the series, both inductive and explanatory methodologies are used.

Each volume in this series presents its author's understanding of the biblical book being studied. As such, it does not necessarily represent the "official" position of the Seventh-day Adventist Church.

It should be noted that the Bible Amplifier series utilizes the New International Version of the Bible as its basic text. *Every reader should read the "How to Use This Book" section to get the fullest benefit from the Bible Amplifier Volumes.*

Dr. William Johnsson, editor of the *Adventist Review*, is uniquely qualified to develop this volume on the book of Hebrews in the Bible Amplifier series. Not only was his doctoral dissertation at Vanderbilt University on the Epistle to the Hebrews, but he has previously published three books on the subject. Dr. Johnsson is a prolific writer. Prior to assuming his present position, he was a pastor and a college and seminary Bible teacher in India and the United States.

George R. Knight

AUTHOR'S PREFACE

Coming back to the book of Hebrews is like visiting a dear friend. I have spent more time with this book than with any other portion of the Bible—in my doctoral dissertation, which centered on chapters 9 and 10; in teaching college and seminary classes for many years; in meetings for ministers; and in writing. Yet I find that Hebrews is an inexhaustible mine of spiritual treasure, and every time I speak or write about it I discover something new that warms my heart.

The book of Hebrews has profoundly impacted my life. I hope this treatment, the fruitage of more than thirty years of reflection, will convey to readers some of the joy, assurance, and practical value that I have found. For Hebrews speaks to our day—of this I am convinced. Hebrews addresses powerfully the spiritual lethargy that grips individual Christians and many congregations. Hebrews pulls us out of the rut of spiritual indifference by directing our gaze to Jesus, whose person and work it uplifts in a presentation of unsurpassed clarity and beauty.

Chitra Barnabas typed and retyped this manuscript, and I am indebted to her for countless hours of faithful labor. And many others—who knows how many hundreds and thousands from classrooms, seminars, camp meetings, ministers' meetings, or by letter—have shared their reactions and insights on the marvelous book of Hebrews. To everyone who has enriched my understanding, helped me see fresh perspectives, or corrected my ideas, I am deeply grateful. Most of all, however, I thank my Lord, who has given me the opportunity to spend so many hours with this precious book.

William G. Johnsson
Silver Spring, Maryland

How to Use This Book

The Abundant Life Bible Amplifier series treats each major portion of each Bible book in five main sections.

The first section is called "Getting Into the Word." The purpose of this section is to encourage readers to study their own Bibles. For that reason, the text of the Bible has not been printed in the volumes in this series.

You will get the most out of your study if you work through the exercises in each of the "Getting Into the Word" sections. This will not only aid you in learning more about the Bible but will also increase your skill in using Bible tools and in asking (and answering) meaningful questions about the Bible.

It will be helpful if you write out the answers and keep them in a notebook or file folder for each biblical book. Writing out your thoughts will enhance your understanding. The benefit derived from such study, of course, will be proportionate to the amount of effort expended.

The "Getting Into the Word" sections assume that the reader has certain minimal tools available. Among these are a concordance and a Bible with maps and marginal cross-references. If you don't have a New International Version of the Bible, we recommend that you obtain one for use with this series, since all the Bible Amplifier authors are using the NIV as their basic text. For the same reason, your best choice of a concordance is the *NIV*

Exhaustive Concordance, edited by E. W. Goodrick and J. R. Kohlenberger. *Strong's Exhaustive Concordance of the Bible* and Young's *Analytical Concordance to the Bible* are also useful. However, even if all you have is Cruden's Concordance, you will be able to do all of the "Getting Into the Word" exercises and most of the "Researching the Word" exercises.

The "Getting Into the Word" sections also assume that the reader has a Bible dictionary. The *Seventh-day Adventist Bible Dictionary* is quite helpful, but those interested in greater depth may want to acquire the four-volume *International Standard Bible Encyclopedia* (1974-1988 edition) or the six-volume *Anchor Bible Dictionary*.

The second section in the treatment of the biblical passages is called "Exploring the Word." The purpose of this section is to discuss the major themes in each biblical book. Thus the comments will typically deal with fairly large portions of Scripture (often an entire chapter) rather than providing a verse-by-verse treatment, such as is found in the *Seventh-day Adventist Bible Commentary*. In fact, many verses and perhaps whole passages in some biblical books may be treated minimally or passed over altogether.

Another thing that should be noted is that the purpose of the "Exploring the Word" sections is not to respond to all the problems or answer all the questions that might arise in each passage. Rather, as stated above, the "Exploring the Word" sections are to develop the Bible writers' major themes. In the process, the author of each volume will bring the best of modern scholarship into the discussion and thus enrich the reader's understanding of the biblical passage at hand. The "Exploring the Word" sections will also develop and provide insight into many of the issues first raised in the "Getting Into the Word" exercises.

The third section in the treatment of the biblical passages is "Applying the Word." This section is aimed at bringing the lessons of each passage into daily life. Once again, you may want to write out a response to these questions and keep them in your notebook or file folder on the biblical book being studied.

The fourth section, "Researching the Word," is for those students who want to delve more deeply into the Bible passage under study or into the history behind it. It is recognized that not everyone will have the research tools for this section. Those expecting to use the research sections should have an exhaustive Bible concordance, the *Seventh-day Adventist Bible Commentary*, a good Bible dictionary, and a Bible atlas. It also will be helpful to have several versions of the Bible.

The final component in each chapter of this book will be a list of recommendations for "Further Study on the Word." While most readers will not have all of these works, many of them may be available in local libraries. Others can be purchased through your local book dealer. It is assumed that many users of this series will already own the seven-volume *Seventh-day Adventist Bible Commentary* and the one-volume *Seventh-day Adventist Bible Dictionary*.

In closing, it should be noted that while a reader will learn much about the Bible from a *reading* of the books in the Bible Amplifier series, he or she will gain infinitely more by *studying* the Bible in connection with that reading.

The Book of Hebrews

Before studying what anyone has written about the book of Hebrews, listen to the book itself. Take your Bible—preferably the New International Version, since we will be using that—and open to Hebrews. Read the entire document at one sitting. It isn't as long as you might think; all you need is about one hour.

As you begin to read, pray that the Lord will open your eyes so that you may see and understand. In addition:

1. **List on a piece of paper what you consider to be the main point or idea of each chapter. Try to see how each chapter builds on the one before so that the book comes together as a whole.**
2. **What do you think is the theme of the book as a whole? What problems or issues in the Christian community to whom the author was writing do you think he may have been trying to help them with?**
3. **For each chapter, list or underline one text or idea that speaks especially to your spiritual life at this time. Why does the text or thought seem so precious to you?**

The book of Hebrews amazes and mystifies. To many Christians, including those who spend much time with the Bible, the book remains remote. They marvel at the majesty of its concepts and the power of its logic, but its language of priests and temples,

17

of sacrifices and ceremonial purifications, seems to belong to another age.

Not surprisingly, modern biblical scholarship has largely neglected Hebrews. Whereas a century ago giants like Bishop W. H. Westcott produced masterly commentaries on this book, the writings of recent times have been puny, stilted. Only in the past thirty years or so have Protestant scholars begun to do serious work in Hebrews again.

And what about Seventh-day Adventists? Hebrews, because of its teaching about the high-priestly ministry of Jesus and the heavenly sanctuary, played a major role in the formation of Adventist doctrine. Sadly, we, too, have neglected this book in recent times. We have largely failed to take the time to listen and to understand, to stay with the text long enough that the Holy Spirit can reveal its meaning and its message for our day.

Hebrews isn't an easy book, though neither is it as difficult as we may think. If we study it as a *whole*—starting at the beginning, following the argument in its measured, magnificent development, letting the Word speak to us first in its terms and not ours—we can grasp its meaning.

Hebrews contains a word from the Lord for us. Hebrews *is* the Word of the Lord. Because it is, we will find this ancient writing intellectually stimulating, spiritually rewarding— and surprisingly contemporary in its message.

The Structure of Hebrews

What stands out in your mind from your reading of Hebrews? Set aside, for now, questions you may have; did you see any pattern or structure in the emerging argument of the book?

For instance, did you notice how, from time to time, the discussion about Jesus—who He is and His high-priestly work—stops for practical applications? The theological argument breaks periodically for practical application. These breaks are signaled by words like *therefore* (2:1; 3:1; 10:19), and by the abrupt change from the third person to the first or second person. That is, Hebrews alternates theological discussion with practical application. People often think of Hebrews as a book heavy with theological reasoning, but the theology over and over merges with application to life. We may discern the following pattern:

Argument	1:1-14
Application	2:1-4
Argument	2:5–3:6a
Application	3:6b–4:13
Argument	5:1-10
Application	5:11–6:20
Argument	7:1–10:18
Application	10:19–13:25

This structure is unique in Scripture. To appreciate its full force, we must realize that more than alternation is involved. Both theological argument and practical application build in length and power as they proceed, each reaching its own climax. At the same time, each matches and blends with the other.

A thousand miles from the ocean, the Rio Negro joins the mighty Amazon. The Amazon runs fast, brown, and massive; the Negro's waters are clear, with a blackish tint. The rivers join and merge, but for miles they run side by side. As you look down from an airplane, you can see the Negro waters in the midst of the Amazon.

That is like Hebrews. Two streams but one river; two currents, each developing its own course, but one work with one purpose. What a masterpiece!

Another feature of Hebrews is the careful development of major ideas. One by one each is introduced, fleshed out, and then rounded off. For instance, the high-priestly concept is introduced at 2:17, 18, expanded at 4:14–5:10, and fully developed at 7:1–10:18. Covenant is introduced at 7:22, developed in 8:6-13, and wound up at 10:16-18. Likewise faith, introduced at 2:17, is expanded in 3:1-6 but only treated fully in 11:1-39.

A third feature of the structure is the manner in which Psalm

110 influences the theological argumentation. We find an allusion to the opening verse of the psalm as early as Hebrews 1:4, then later references in 1:13; 8:1; 10:12, 13; and 12:2.

But the fourth verse of the psalm—"The Lord has sworn and will not change his mind: 'You are a priest forever, in the order of Melchizedek' "—plays a crucial role. This scripture provides the primary Old Testament anticipation of the high-priestly idea, and the author of Hebrews takes it up point by point in his argument. In Hebrews 5:5, 6 this verse is used to show divine appointment to the priesthood; in 6:19, 20 that Jesus has become a high priest; in 7:11, 12 to show divine prediction of a new order of priesthood; in 7:15-17 that Christ's priesthood is for ever; and in 7:20, 21 that the divine oath sets apart His office.

The Purpose of Hebrews

The writer calls his work a "word of exhortation" (13:22). He did not intend it to be a theological treatise divorced from life, and our studies of structure have shown well that point. Theology and application dovetail into one another, as theological argument serves the application and the application arises out of the argument.

We best understand Hebrews, therefore, as a sermon. As in all good preaching, the pastor has an aim in view. He or she speaks to a spiritual need. But preaching isn't haranguing the people; preaching has a theological base. Exhortation only becomes effective when it proceeds from a foundation of Scripture and theological reasoning.

What, then, was the preacher's purpose in the sermon to the Hebrews? The applications give us the answer. As we work through the passages we located under structure, we learn the faults in the congregation and the preacher's admonitions to his people in view of those faults. Out of it all we get a pretty clear spiritual profile of the people.

They had been Christians for quite some time and could recall the preaching of the apostles and miracles associated with the gifts of the Holy Spirit (2:3,4). In the early years of their faith, they had suffered insults, persecution, and even confiscation of their property; they had stood side by side with those imprisoned for Christ (10:32,34).

But the years have rolled on; now they have grown weary in the Christian way. They feel like letting go, simply drifting away with the crowd (2:1). They have begun to neglect the faith (2:2); they feel tempted to unbelief (3:2-14). Sin's deceitfulness has begun to harden their hearts (3:13-16); they have failed to grow spiritually (5:11-14). They gradually quit coming to church (10:25), and some may even have publicly renounced Christ (6:4-6; 10:26-31; 12:15-17).

So the "problem" of the Hebrew Christians is either a *weariness* leading to gradual drifting away from the community, or a deliberate, open *rejection* of Christ and His people because of the inroads of sin in the heart.

Is the preacher talking to them—or to us? The spiritual profile of the Hebrews bears startling resemblances to Christians today.

The "solution" corresponds to the problem. The preacher admonishes the people to stay alert (2:1), to hold fast (3:6, 14; 10:23), to grasp (4:14; 6:18), to be earnest (4:11; 6:11), to consider (3:1), to exhort one another (3:13; 10:25; 13:19, 22), to recall (10:32), and to endure (10:36; 12:1).

The great quality held out, however, is faith. Faith characterized the life of both Jesus and Moses (3:2); lack of faith led to Israel's failure (4:12). The heroes of old overcame physical hardships and conquered temptations through faith (11:1-39), and so will Christians of the first century—and even today.

But the admonitions grow out of theology, as we have seen—and that theology boils down to the *magnificence of Jesus and His work for us*. "Such a great salvation" (2:3)—this is what it will all come down to. If the tired Hebrew Christians can catch a glimpse of their Lord—who He is, what He accomplished on Calvary, His heavenly ministry—they will no longer neglect or reject the faith. They will be renewed, revived, invigorated.

And so will we.

Hebrews' Major Themes

1. *The magnificence of Jesus* dominates the thought patterns of the book. All the applications spring from this truth; they aren't merely a preacher's concern to hold his flock together. Jesus! He is the One altogether magnificent—magnificent in His person, magnificent in His work. Hebrews develops the portrait of Jesus as High Priest like no other portion of Scripture. Elsewhere we find the idea barely alluded to or suggested, as in Romans (8:34) or John (1 John 2:1, 2) or Revelation (1:12-20); in Hebrews we see it argued systematically (2:17, 18; 4:14–5:10; 6:20–8:2).

But Hebrews presents other portraits of Jesus—not so extensively as the high-priestly one, but nonetheless significant. Jesus is the *pioneer* who has passed over life's course of suffering and temptation (2:10; 12:2); He is also the *apostle* of our faith (2:1) who was sent to earth for us and the *forerunner* (6:20) who has gone on ahead to the heavenly courts.

2. *Full assurance in Jesus.* The Hebrew Christians, a despised, persecuted minority, had privileges beyond the Jerusalem temple and its rituals—if only they could have seen them. The Lord Jesus was the true High Priest, and He ministered in the true temple—the heavenly one, of which the earthly was but a weak reflection. His sacrifice of Himself on Calvary accomplished at a stroke something that all the slaying of animals could never do—it purged sins, once for all.

So in Jesus Christians have full assurance. They have access to the heavenly Most Holy Place and a conscience cleansed of sin.

> Therefore, brothers, since we have confidence to enter the Most Holy Place by the blood of Jesus, by a new and living way opened for us through the curtain, that is, his body, and since we have a great high priest over the house of God, let us draw near to God with a sincere heart in full assurance of faith, having our hearts sprinkled to cleanse us from a guilty conscience and having our bodies washed with pure water (Heb. 10:19-22).

3. Sin, however, is an exceedingly serious thing. The absolute confidence that Christians may have in Jesus doesn't take sin lightly. Sin cost the death of the spotless Son of God. So heavy is it that no manner or number of rituals and animal sacrifices could ever bring remission (9:6-10; 10:1-4). These bloody sacrifices were but types and shadows of what Jesus would accomplish by His dying (10:1, 2).

In three striking passages (6:4-6; 10:26-31; 12:15-17), the author lays on the line the seriousness of neglecting or rejecting Jesus. So strong is his language that Christians have debated their meaning from the earliest centuries. The point in all three is the same: In view of the magnificence of Jesus and His work, how heinous to abandon Him and His saving blood.

4. Christian life as pilgrimage also runs through this book. Throughout history, God's followers have been strangers and aliens on this earth. They have looked beyond the pleasures of this world, because they have an eternal destiny. Whatever hardships, insults, and difficulties they have encountered, they know that they are citizens of a better country. Like Abraham, they see their life on earth as merely a sojourn, a series of stages on the way to their goal—the heavenly Jerusalem (11:13-16).

5. Faith emerges as the quality above all others to characterize God's pilgrim people. Hebrews 11 is rightly famous for its parade of men and women of faith; but, in fact, faith is underlined throughout the book. Faith has two elements: It sees the unseen, and it turns hope into reality. Faith is active and dynamic; it endures patiently. Faith is faithful.

6. The Sabbath plays a distinct and unique role in Hebrews as a symbol of our rest in Christ. The argument in 3:6–4:10 will reward our careful study with insights regarding the place of the Sabbath in early Christianity and the theological significance of the Sabbath.

7. The second coming. The book of Hebrews, so strong in developing the pilgrimage idea and the heavenly work of Christ, also points to *"the* Day" (10:25)—the day of the Lord that will usher Christian pilgrims into their eternal rest.

Indeed, Christ's *past* work (Calvary) and His *present* work (intercession) guarantee His *future* coming. "Just as man is destined to die once, and after that to face judgment, so Christ was sacrificed once to take away the sins of many people; and he will appear a second time, not to bear sin, but to bring salvation to those who are waiting for him" (9:27, 28). Though the way may seem long for the Christian pilgrim, "in just a very little while He who is coming will come and will not delay" (10:37). He who once shook the earth at the giving of the law on Mount Sinai will once again shake it—and not only the earth but the heavens also (12:26, 27).

Outline of Hebrews

   I. The Magnificence of Jesus (1:1-4)
     The better revelation
  II. The Magnificence of Jesus' Person (1:5–7:28)
     A. The better name (1:5–2:18)
     B. The better leader (3:1–4:13)
     C. The better priest (4:14–6:20)
     D. The better priesthood (7:1-28)
 III. The Magnificence of Jesus' Work (8:1–10:18)
     A. The better covenant (8:1–9:10)
     B. The better blood (9:11–10:18)
 IV. Living in View of Jesus' Achievement (10:19–13:25)
     A. The better country (10:19–11:40)
     B. The better city (12:1–13:25)

The Perennial Question

In many years of teaching the book of Hebrews, I have heard one question above all others: Who wrote it?

In the King James Version the superscription to the book reads, "The Epistle of Paul the Apostle to the Hebrews." Those words, however, were added after several centuries; the oldest title is simply "To the Hebrews."

In fact, every point of the King James Version superscription has been challenged. Hebrews bears almost none of the usual marks of a letter—designation of the sender, the readers, an opening greeting, and personal matters. It is, as we have seen, a written sermon rather than an epistle.

Likewise, the identity of the readers has been called into question, with several scholars favoring a Gentile audience. On balance, however, I think the evidence points to Jewish Christians feeling the pain of rejection by their fellow countrymen and perhaps exclusion from the rituals of their ancestral faith.

But still the question—who wrote it? Because the author did not identify himself, speculation has abounded. We know that as early as the second century, Christians were discussing the authorship of Hebrews. In the 190s Clement of Alexandria concluded that Paul wrote it in the Hebrew language, while Luke translated it into Greek.

However, a few years later, the scholar Origen left the matter open-ended:

> If I gave my opinion, I should say that the thoughts are those of the apostle, but the diction and phraseology are those of someone who remembered the apostolic teachings and wrote down at his leisure what had been said by his teacher. Therefore if any church holds that this epistle is by Paul, let it be commended for this. For not without reason have the ancients handed it down as Paul's. But who wrote the epistle, in truth, God knows. The statement of some who have gone before us is that Clement, bishop of Romans, wrote the epistle, and of others that Luke, the author of the Gospel and the Acts, wrote it. But let this suffice on these matters (Eusebius, *Ecclesiastical History*, 6:25).

These questions help explain one of the most puzzling facts of the early church: Hebrews was one of the last books to be accepted into the New Testament canon. For a book to be considered canonical, it had to come from the hand of an apostle or someone associated with an apostle. Only after several hundred years did the view of Pauline authorship prevail and Hebrews find universal acceptance.

But surely Paul is the logical candidate for author? If not Paul, who?

I am wary of arguments from silence. Just as I reject the contention that Paul *must* have written Hebrews because he was the only one capable of this masterpiece, I also reject the view that Paul could *not* have written Hebrews—which is what most scholars, including conservatives, hold today. They point to major differences of language (the Greek of Hebrews is unlike that of Paul in his letters) and ideas. For instance, the author of Hebrews doesn't speak of himself as an apostle (2:3, 4; 13:6, 7), and he uses terms like *law* and *faith* in ways quite different from Romans and Galatians.

Seventh-day Adventists have an unusual interest in the question of authorship. Ellen G. White, whom we believe to have received the prophetic gift, attributes the book to Paul in many incidental references. Sometimes, however, she simply refers to "the apostle."

While I recognize the differences from Paul's acknowledged writings, I also find resonances with those writings in the book of Hebrews. I think the book is Pauline, but with some other factor associated with its writing that was quickly lost. To me, this makes far better sense of the data than speculating that Luke or Peter or Apollos or Prisca (Priscilla) wrote it. The essential question, however, is clear beyond dispute: This book is *inspired*, a work of the Holy Spirit that speaks with power to Christians today—and to me.

A final question: When? While we cannot establish the point with certainty, much of the reasoning suggests a date in the 60s. M. L. Andreasen argued strongly for a context in which Jewish Christians faced the imminent loss of the temple, and his logic retains force. And a date in the early 60s, of course, supports a Pauline link for the book.

For Further Reading

1. M. L. Andreasen, *The Book of Hebrews*.
2. F. F. Bruce, *The Epistle to the Hebrews*, rev. ed., xix-xxii.
3. P. E. Hughes, *A Commentary on the Epistle to the Hebrews*, 1-32.
4. W. G. Johnsson, *In Absolute Confidence*, 9-33.
5. *Seventh-day Adventist Bible Commentary*, F. D. Nichol, ed. 7:387-394.
6. *Seventh-day Adventist Bible Dictionary*.
7. B. F. Westcott, *The Epistle to the Hebrews*, xxvii-1xxxiv.

LIST OF WORKS CITED

Andreasen, M. L. The Book of *Hebrews*. Washington, D.C.: Review and Herald, 1948.

Ballenger, Albion Foss. *Cast Out for the Cross of Christ*. Tropico, Calif.: Published by author, n.d.

Bruce, F. F. *The Epistle to the Hebrews*. Revised Edition. Grand Rapids, Mich.: Eerdmans, 1990.

_____. *The Spreading Flame*. Grand Rapids, Mich.: Eerdmans, 1961.

Canright, D. M. *Seventh-day Adventism Renounced*. Chicago: Fleming H. Revell, 1889.

Davidson, Richard M. "Typology in the Book of Hebrews." In *Issues in the Book of Hebrews*, edited by Frank B. Holbrook (Daniel and Revelation Committee Series, vol. 4). Silver Spring, Md.: General Conference of Seventh-day Adventists, 1989.

Horn, Siegfried H., et. al. *Seventh-day Adventist Bible Dictionary*. Washington, D.C.: Review and Herald, 1960.

Hughes, Philip Edgcumbe. *A Commentary on the Epistle to the Hebrews*. Grand Rapids, Mich.: Eerdmans, 1977.

Johnsson, William G. "Day of Atonement Allusions." In *Issues in the Book of Hebrews*, edited by Frank B. Holbrook (Daniel and Revelation Committee Series, vol. 4). Silver Spring, Md.: General Conference of Seventh-day Adventists, 1989.

_____. "The Heavenly Sanctuary—Figurative or Real?" In *Issues in the Book of Hebrews*, edited by Frank B. Holbrook (Daniel and Revelation Committee Series, vol. 4). Silver Spring, Md.: General Conference of Seventh-day Adventists, 1989.

_____. "Defilement/Purification and Hebrews 9:23." In *Issues in the Book of Hebrews*, edited by Frank B. Holbrook (Daniel and Revelation Committee Series, vol. 4). Silver Spring, Md.: General Conference of Seventh-day Adventists, 1989.

_____. *In Absolute Confidence*. Nashville, Tenn.: Southern Publishing Association, 1979.

Kiesler, Herbert. "An Exegesis of Selected Passages." In *Issues in the Book of Hebrews*, edited by Frank B. Holbrook (Daniel and Revelation Committee Series, vol. 4). Silver Spring, Md.: General Conference of Seventh-day Adventists, 1989.

Moffatt, James. *A Critical and Exegetical Commentary on the Epistle to the Hebrews*. Edinburgh: T. & T. Clark, 1968.

_____. "*Ta Hagia* in the Epistle to the Hebrews." *Andrews University Studies* 5 (January 1967), 59-70.

Nichol, Francis D., ed. *Seventh-day Adventist Bible Commentary*, 7 vols. Washington, D.C.: Review and Herald, 1953-1957, 1976-1980.

Salom, Alwyn P. "Sanctuary Theology." In *Issues in the Book of Hebrews*, edited by Frank B. Holbrook (Daniel and Revelation Committee Series, vol. 4). Silver Spring, Md.: General Conference of Seventh-day Adventists, 1989.

Smith, Uriah. *The Advent Review and Sabbath Herald*, 5 Nov. 1895.

Treiyer, Alberto R. "Antithetical or Correspondence Typology?" In *Issues in the Book of Hebrews*, edited by Frank B. Holbrook (Daniel and Revelation Committee Series, vol. 4). Silver Spring, Md.: General Conference of Seventh-day Adventists.

Wallenkampf, Arnold V. "A Brief Review of Some of the Internal and External Challengers to the SDA Teachings on the Sanctuary and the Atonement." In *The Sanctuary and the Atonement*, edited by Arnold V. Wallenkampf and W. Richard Lesher. Washington, D.C.: Review and Herald, 1981.

Westcott, Brooke Foss. *The Epistle to the Hebrews*. Grand Rapids, Mich.: Eerdmans, 1965.

White, Ellen G. *Counsels to Parents, Teachers, and Students Regarding Christian Education*. Boise, Idaho: Pacific Press, 1943.

_____. *The Desire of Ages*. Boise, Idaho: Pacific Press, 1940.

_____. *Evangelism*. Washington, D.C.: Review and Herald, 1946.

_____. *The Great Controversy Between Christ and Satan*. Boise, Idaho: Pacific Press, 1950.

_____. *Selected Messages*. Book 1. Washington, D.C.: Review and

Herald, 1958.

_____. *Testimonies for the Church*. Vol. 7. Boise, Idaho: Pacific Press, 1948.

_____. "Search the Scriptures," *The Youth's Instructor*, 13 Oct. 1898.

PART ONE

The Magnificence
of Jesus

Hebrews 1:1-4

CHAPTER ONE

The Better Revelation

Hebrews 1:1-4

The book of Hebrews opens with a dramatic flourish, as arresting and compelling as the da-da-da-dah *that launches Beethoven's Fifth Symphony. We hear heavenly music—ideas that grasp us by the hand and wrench us out of our mundane world and into the courts of the living God. Four magnificent verses propel us into the thought of this powerful document.*

These verses form more than an introduction or prelude to what follows. Rather, we best listen to them as an overture, sounding the great themes that the apostle will develop at length in the course of his sermon. The words, the ideas, rise and fall, weaving and blending, moving forward relentlessly. They don't form an outline—he won't subsequently take them up in order— but rather a thematic cascade, a tone poem of extraordinary richness.

As powerful as we find these verses in our English Bible, the original Greek text is even stronger. The New International Version divides the passages into four sentences, but as it came from the apostle's hand it was but one, a carefully crafted literary unit with point and counterpoint, theme echoing theme, resonating and rising to the throne of God like a grand orchestral composition.

These verses will reward our careful study. To listen to their music will help us catch the spirit of Hebrews; to contemplate their themes will prepare us for a theological feast; and to see their intent will bring us face to face with Jesus in His magnificence.

■ Getting Into the Word

Hebrews 1:1-4

Read through Hebrews 1:1-4 several times. Look at different translations, including the King James Version and the New International Version. Read slowly and prayerfully, listening for the music and trying to catch the major themes. Then respond to the following questions:

1. Think about the way other books of the Bible begin. Look at Genesis 1 and John 1 in particular. Compare and contrast the beginning of Hebrews with these books.
2. Who seems to be the subject of Hebrews 1:1-4? Remember, in the original, this is one sustained sentence; so is God or the Son the chief point of interest? Explain your answer.
3. What does the author mean by God's "speaking"? Does he intend only the spoken word that can be heard by human ears? Draw up a list of the "many times" and "various ways" in which God spoke in the Old Testament.
4. List the various qualities and activities of the Son in Hebrews 1:1-40. Using a concordance, look up other references to "son" in Hebrews, and study these occurrences in an endeavor to probe the meaning of this key word. By reason of the Incarnation, Jesus is obviously God's Son, but does Hebrews indicate a deeper meaning? For instance, some commentators (and the statement of fundamental beliefs of Seventh-day Adventists) refer to Christ's *eternal* Sonship. Does Hebrews support this conclusion? In what sense or senses might this be true?
5. Notice the manner in which Jesus' work is set forth in the passage. Think about the biblical functions of prophet, priest, and king. What evidence do you see here that Jesus fulfills each of these functions?
6. Contemplate also the themes of Hebrews 1:1-4 with reference to Jesus before and after the Incarnation. In what

ways is the "old" (before Christ) different from the "new" (after Christ)? Does Paul put down the Old Testament? In what ways did the Son's coming to earth make a difference?

7. The writer obviously had to condense the work of the Son during His earthly sojourn. What did he omit? Why? What is his focus?

8. With the help of a concordance, look up the various references to "better" and "superior" in Hebrews. Does this suggest to you a theme for the book?

9. Read Hebrews 1:1-4 one more time. You understand it better now, but you no doubt have many questions—you want to know more. The answers will come from Hebrews itself as we work through it, listening to the music of the text. From this initial study, however, you have begun to form conclusions. From these opening verses, what would you expect the rest of the book to be about? Reflect for a moment on the effect they have had on you. Jot down your reflections.

■ Exploring the Word

The God Who Speaks

Hebrews opens with two fundamental, life-transforming statements: God is, and God speaks. All that follows hangs on these affirmations.

We can neither prove nor disprove these statements. They are presuppositions, the building blocks of the universe of thought. We can, however, suggest evidence that supports them.

God—before all else is said. God—above all, beyond all. God—in all, through all, to all. Here our thought begins, and of Him will our last thought be.

We were made for Him, made by Him, and, as Augustine said, we are restless until we find our rest in Him. We who believe know Him as Friend—our truest Companion who sticks closer than a brother. Although we have never seen Him, we love Him and rejoice in Him with unspeakable, glorious joy (1 Pet. 1:8).

Yet we cannot *prove* that God exists. For centuries philosophers and theologians have sought out rational arguments, reasoning from the nature of existence or the evidences of design or the moral aspects of our being. All these arguments are helpful, but none can quite clinch the case. The atheist lines up his ducks also, and in the end each side cancels out the other.

"The person who comes to God must *believe* that He exists," the apostle will tell us later (11:6). That is the way we come to know Him and continue to grow in Him—by faith. And it is the only way.

For God is too big for human "proof." Too big to be established by scientific experimentation. Too big for logic and rational argument. God is the Mind that made all and maintains all, the Mind that our mind feebly echoes. No human mind can fully grasp the divine Mind.

But we who believe see His footprints everywhere. To us, this world is His world, and we are His children. While we cannot explain why everything happens just as it does—especially the tragic and the ugly—we have confidence that we are secure in His hands.

As God is the first and major assumption of Hebrews, so He is the backdrop for all that happens in the book. Or, to change the image, although the Son is the figure in the spotlight, the soloist for the concerto, God conducts the orchestra that supplies the harmony. We find the name *God* sixty-seven times in this book. Twelve times we hear *Lord* instead. These uses derive from the apostle's references to the Septuagint, the Greek translation of the Old Testament. But not once do we find *Father.*

God, we learn, is the founder of all (3:4). He wills the sufferings and death of the Son (2:10), appoints Moses to service (3:2-5), Aaron to high-priestly office (5:4), and Jesus as High Priest of a new order (5:5). God made all things by His word (11:3). He gives promises to humanity, adding an oath to make our future absolutely certain (6:17, 18). God brings blessings and curses (6:7,

8), provides grace (4:16), and remembers acts of loving service (6:10). He gives peace (13:20), warns (13:25), and delivers from death (5:7; 11:19).

And God draws near to humankind, entering into covenant relation with His people (8:8). The apostle calls us a "household" (3:6)—a family lovingly disciplined by the divine Parent (12:3-11). But God is a "consuming fire" to those who despise His grace (12:29).

God's major activity, however, is speaking. That is the second assumption we find in the book's opening words, and we will hear it throughout. We find God "speaking" or "saying" (a different verb in the original)—fourteen times in Hebrews for the former, twenty-two for the latter, making a total of thirty-six references throughout the book.

God's speaking creates the universe (1:3). It designates the Son as superior to angels (1:5-14). It warns us against falling away from the divine purpose (3:7-15). And it guarantees fulfillment of the divine plan (4:1-10).

"At many times and in various ways"—this is how Hebrews 1:1 describes God's speaking. Think of the *times* of the Old Testament—the ongoing, repeated, periodic divine communication. "And God said." This is how the Creation takes place. God spoke to our first parents, Adam and Eve, in the garden; to Cain, the first murderer, and to Noah, the preacher of righteousness; to Abram, in pagan Ur of the Chaldees, and to Jacob, fleeing from his angry brother; and to Moses and Malachi, Samson and Samuel, David and Deborah, Jeremiah and Jehu, Ezekiel and Esther. Throughout the Old Testament, from its first chapter to its last, Yahweh is the God who speaks.

Think, too, of the *ways* of the divine speaking. In Eden, face to face; from Sinai, with thunder, lightning, and trumpet blast; at the tabernacle in Shiloh, a call in the night to a young boy on his bed (1 Sam. 3:1-14); to Jeremiah, feeling a fire in his bones (Jer. 20:9); to Isaiah, as he enters the temple to worship (Isa. 6:1-4); to Daniel, far from home in a captor's land (Dan. 10:1-14); and forty days later, in a "still, small voice" to the hero of Mount Carmel

(1 Kings 19:12, KJV).

God's speaking cannot be circumscribed or predicted. We cannot know *when* or *how* God will speak, but we can be sure that He *will* speak. He can speak to a prophet through dreams and visions, but He can also use a beast—a donkey!—to rebuke that same fellow when he embarks on a wrong course of action (Num. 22:28).

What does God's "speaking" mean? Yes, words, actual speech; but more than words that enter our ears. God's words may come on stone tablets, or they may fall upon our inward ears, piercing our conscience and complacency in ways that we alone hear them.

Hebrews 1:1, 2 tells us that God spoke "through" or "by." The Greek preposition here is *en*, literally "in." God spoke not only *by* words but *in* His messengers. The total force of their lives conveyed God's will: they lived out His message.

Thus, God's speaking connotes His total communication. Audible words, written words, silent words, but living words—God speaks. From the beginning, He speaks; He keeps speaking to each generation; He never ceases to speak.

And we of faith affirm: God speaks today. God hasn't left us to grope alone in a silent universe. He hasn't abandoned us to doubts and despair. He speaks: He speaks today.

This truth of the God who speaks is one of the most precious ideas of Scripture. It means much to me. It means that each child of God may feel a hand in his or hers, may hear a voice along life's road: "This is the way; walk in it" (Isa. 30:21).

I cannot tell you *when* or *how* God will speak. God is God, not subject to our wishes or limited to our methods. But God loves us and wants to help us. He desires to communicate with us, to ease our burdens, to guide us through the perplexities and worries that tear us apart. When we cast all our burdens on Him, as He invites us to (1 Pet. 5:7), we may confidently expect an answer. But in His time, and in His way.

> The Lord will teach us our duty just as willingly as
> He will teach somebody else. If we come to Him in faith,
> He will speak His mysteries to us personally. Our hearts

will often burn within us as One draws nigh to com-
mune with us as He did with Enoch. Those who decide
to do nothing in any line that will displease God, will
know, after presenting their case before Him, just what
course to pursue. And they will receive not only wisdom, but strength (White, *The Desire of Ages*, 668).

The God who speaks—what a startling, revolutionary idea to
human beings on the threshold of the new millennium! Kafka,
Hemingway, Russell, Sartre—these voices have shaped the twentieth century, and they portrayed human existence as "a dirty joke"
(Hemingway), devoid of meaning (Kafka and Sartre), or "built
upon the platform of unyielding despair" (Russell).

But we who believe know otherwise. We know that God speaks.
No, we cannot *prove* it by a cold, "scientific" method. But we know
that He does, because we know Him.

Only two other books of Scripture open with a dramatic flourish like Hebrews. One is Genesis, whose initial words, "In the
beginning God created the heavens and the earth," introduce the
reader to the God who creates.

The other is the Gospel of John, which commences, "In the
beginning was the Word, and the Word was with God, and the
Word was God. He was with God in the beginning." These words
take us back prior to Genesis 1:1, to the beginning of beginnings,
the beginning before all beginnings, back beyond the creation of
our world, as far as our minds can stretch. In that "beginning"—
God! Before all else, Source of all else—God!

And, interestingly, alongside God in the beginning is the Word.
What God is, the Word is.

Hebrews 1:1-4 catches up these ideas of Genesis 1 and John 1
(although John's Gospel was likely written later than Hebrews)
and pulls them together. The first assumption is the same for all
three passages—God. But in Hebrews the divine activity, recall-
ing the mysterious "Word," comes to us as speaking rather than
creating.

The apostle's concentration on the divine communication goes beyond affirmation of the many and varied ways of God's speech, however. His argument focuses the divine speech, pointing to a summit, a climax, when, to use John's expression, "the Word became flesh" (John 1:14). This leads us to consider the role and function of the Son in Hebrews 1:1-4.

Finality Through the Son

The first two verses of Hebrews set out a pattern of God's speaking, balancing the old revelation against the new, with point-by-point correspondence in each.

The God Who Speaks

God spoke	He has spoken
to our forefathers	to us
in the past	in these last days
through the prophets.	by His Son.

Only one phrase has no matching words: "At many times and in various ways." The omission hits us even harder in the original because the apostle placed these words at the very first of the book. His actual phrase is *polumerōs kai polutropōs*—Greek words that have a grand and resonant ring in keeping with the sweep of ideas about to be introduced. (The King James Version captures more effectively the dramatic beginning: "God, who at sundry times and in divers manners spake in times past unto the fathers by the prophets.")

This construction—putting "at many times and in various ways" at the very beginning of Hebrews and then not supplying any corresponding phrase—suggests a strong contrast between the old revelation and the new. Whereas the old came in fragments, the new comes with finality. The former was partial; here a little, there a little; the new is complete, perfect.

This is because the new comes by the Son. The description of God's speaking has moved toward this point, and when the Son is introduced, He moves to center stage. So we notice a curious fact about the single long sentence that comprises Hebrews 1:1-4: Although God forms the subject and the book begins with Him, as soon as the Son enters the picture, the remainder, and majority, of the sentence focuses on Him. And that pattern, as we already suggested, continues throughout the book.

"In Son"—that is how the original reads literally. The construction emphasizes the *quality* of Sonship; we bring out the thought better with "by one who is Son," or "by one who has the status of Son." Paul is contrasting the fragmentary revelation that came through prophets with the full revelation that the Son brings.

We will notice the term *Son* several times in Hebrews. Each time the name carries heavy weight, pointing to the significance and superiority of His person. Thus, *Son* indicates revelation with finality (1:2), superiority to angels (1:5-14), qualification for the new and better priesthood (5:4-6; 7:28), and one whom we are warned not to despise (6:6; 10:29). In 2:10-18, the Son takes on our human nature and becomes our brother.

Hebrews 1:1-4 makes three marvelous affirmations concerning the Son. First, He is the radiance of God's glory. The word translated "radiance," *apaugasma*, suggests a beam of light, a bright ray, a shining forth. Various translations render it as "effulgence" (NEB), "brightness" (KJV), "reflection" (RSV), or "radiance" (Phillips). This description lifts us to the realm of glory, where the Son shines in eternal day. He dwells in light unapproachable; He *is* the Light of lights.

He is also the exact representation of God's being. Here the metaphor changes to the seal and its impression on wax. The word is the same as the one from which we derive *character*, and tells us that the Son is the very stamp of the divine essence. What God is, the Son is.

But the affirmation of the Son's glory and deity goes further: The Son *is* the divine radiance and the divine essence. Literally, "being"—not became. Eternally the Son is Light of light. Eternally He is image of the divine. Eternally He has been so. Eternally He will be so.

No more exalted description of the Son can be found in Scripture. Only three other passages compare with these verses in declaring the true, eternal, preexistent deity of our Lord—John 1:1, 2; Colossians 1:15-17; and Revelation 1:5, 17, 18. Here we find the decisive reply to those voices, ancient or modern, who would suggest that He is in some sense less than God or that He was elevated at some point in time to the status of God.

Our salvation hangs on these affirmations and the fact that they declare. Today, as through the centuries, the person of Jesus Christ confronts men and women. He arrests us with His eye and asks us, "Who do *you* say I am?" (Matt. 16:15). We cannot avoid that question. After all the studies in the history of religions, all the psychological analyses and philosophical discourses, the question still stands, demanding our response.

We who believe affirm: Jesus of Nazareth was what He claimed to be. More than a good man, a teacher, a miracle worker. More than the Jews' messiah. Yes, much, much more—God in the flesh! Eternally, truly God!

The term *Son* points to more than the incarnation, though. He did not *become* the Son; He *is* the Son, the eternal Son. *Son* suggests exalted status and function.

Jesus often used this term of Himself. While His most frequent self-designation was "Son of Man," he showed the closeness of His relation to God by *Son*—the word by itself. For instance: "All things have been committed to me by my Father. No one knows the Son except the Father, and no one knows the Father except the Son and those to whom the Son chooses to reveal him" (Matt. 11:27).

The terminology of Father and Son may mislead us. Inevitably we associate it with time and origin: Sons derive their being from fathers; fathers are prior in time. But Jesus as eternal Son did not originate in and through the Father. Rather, the biblical language of Father and Son points to *shared being*, *equality*, *divine essence*. And the Jews so understood this language, for when Jesus called God His own Father, they were offended because they realized He was "making himself equal with God" (John 5:18).

Ellen White's statements about Christ's eternal preexistence and deity run along the same lines. While her "in Christ is life, original, unborrowed, underived" (White, *The Desire of Ages*, 530) has become a classic quote, no less significant is the following:

> The Son is all the fullness of the Godhead manifested. The Word of God declares Him to be the 'express image of His person.' . . .
>
> Christ is the preexistent, self-existent Son of God. . . . In speaking of His preexistence, Christ carries the mind back through dateless ages. He assures us that there never was a time when He was not in close fellowship with the eternal God. He to whose voice the Jews were then listening had been with God as one brought up with Him. . . . He is the eternal, self-existent Son. . . .
>
> While God's Word speaks of the humanity of Christ when upon this earth, it also speaks decidedly regarding His preexistence. The Word existed as a divine being, even as the eternal Son of God, in union and oneness with His Father (White, *Evangelism*, 614, 615).

While affirming the eternal Sonship, Ellen White suggests that the incarnation made Him Son in a different way: "While the Son of a human being, He became the Son of God in a new sense. Thus He stood in our world—the Son of God, yet allied by birth to the human race" (White, *Selected Messages*, 1:227).

Prophet, Priest, and King

The Son's work is as glorious as His person. As we study Hebrews 1:1-4, we see His work in three phrases that correspond to His career—His preincarnate activities, those during the incarnation, and those following.

Preincarnate: The Son created the universe and sustains all things. Not by chance did our world and starry heavens come about; not by chance do they continue. A divine Mind made them, and a divine Hand keeps them turning. And that is the hand that would be nailed to the cross for us. So the world isn't an alien place for the Son—or for us. It's His, and ours.

Incarnate: The entire course of the Son's work on earth is summed up in one clause—"He . . . provided purification for sins." No mention of the Sermon on the Mount or the parables; no miracles, exorcisms, and healings; no temptations; no nurture of the disciples and establishment of the church. The apostle cuts to the root, to the problem that turned humanity from God's will in the garden and still lies back of the suffering, pain, and desperate needs of men and women today.

Postincarnate: The Son sat down at the right hand of the Majesty in heaven. That is, He reigns. Sitting indicates that His work of purifying sins was completed, successful. Now He rules from the place of honor.

But He is heir of all things, meaning that eventually all things will return to Him. By His person as eternal Son He *is* Lord of lords and King of kings; by reason of His creatorship and sustaining power He *has* the right to reign over all—but presently only the church so acknowledges Him. But, because He is heir of all things, the entire universe at last will come back to Him to serve and to worship.

We can break down the understanding of the work of the Son in yet another way. We can see it in terms of prophet, priest, and king.

As Prophet, the Son conveys the divine will. In Him, as we have seen, the speaking of God reaches its zenith. There is no more fragmentary, imperfect communication; now the Word has become flesh. He speaks the words of God; He lives the words of God; He *is* the Word of God. Just before His departure from this earth, when Philip wanted to see the Father, He said: "Don't you know me, Philip, even after I have been among you such a long time? Anyone who has seen me has seen the Father" (John 14:9). "No one has ever seen God, but . . . the . . . Son . . . has made him known" (John 1:18).

As Priest, the . . . Son makes us clean before God. He offers a sacrifice, even Himself, that has more power than a thousand bulls or goats. He deals with our sins, once and for all.

In the New Testament, we find Jesus' saving work portrayed in a variety of ways. For instance, He brings us acquittal in court (justification), buys us back (redemption), puts us in God's family (adoption), and restores our broken relationship with God (reconciliation). But the language of purification in Hebrews 1:3 ties salvation firmly to the sanctuary and its services; and that connection will emerge as the major theological thrust in the development of the book.

As King, the Son now reigns. We serve One who has all power, to whom the heavenly hosts give allegiance. Because He is King, He will return to our world to assume His rightful role over the people He created and won back to God.

The Old Testament generally keeps the roles of prophet, priest, and king separate and distinct. Occasionally certain individuals combined two roles—like Jeremiah, who was a prophet as well as a priest, or David, who was both king and prophet. But no person in the Old Testament was ever prophet, priest, and king—all three. This could have happened only if a king had come from the tribe of Levi (since the priesthood was hereditary), and none ever did.

But the Son is unique. Unique in person, unique in work, He sums up the Old Testament and goes far beyond. In Him all roles reach their climax and find their ultimate meaning.

The Old and the New—Something Better

In this overture to Hebrews, we hear strains of a melody that will sound many times through the book. The apostle compares and contrasts the old and the new—"in the past . . . in these last days." Here he argues that the new revelation is superior to the old because it comes through One who is Son rather than through prophets, and because it comes perfectly rather than fragmentarily.

Note: We aren't dealing with the bad versus the good, but the good versus the better (or the ultimate). The Old Testament isn't flawed or defective—how could it be, since God was its Author? But the Old Testament, good as it was, pointed beyond itself to the One who would come as God's speech embodied; then the partial would become whole.

One of the key words of Hebrews, therefore, is *better*. We find this word a total of thirteen times (1:4; 6:9; 7:7, 19, 22; 8:6; 9:23; 10:34; 11:16, 35, 40; 12:24). Beyond these occurrences, however, the apostle has structured the entire argument around a series of comparisons. The old and the new run together throughout, with the new growing out of the old, building upon it, but surpassing it. So, apart from the better revelation of 1:1-4, we find the better name (1:5-14), the better Leader (3:1-6), the better Priest (4:14–5:10), the better priesthood (7:1-28), the better sanctuary (8:1-6), the better covenant (8:6-13), the better blood (9:1–10:18), the better country (11:13-16), and the better city (12:18-24; 13:14).

As we work through Hebrews, we will need to listen carefully to the intricacies of the melodies of "old" and "new." Many Christians, unfortunately, consider the Old Testament to be a closed book that may safely be neglected, and because of this it fails to speak to their lives today. They err greatly, depriving themselves of spiritual treasure provided by God Himself. Other Christians, including some Adventists, make exactly the opposite mistake: they collapse the new into the old, leveling out its distinctiveness, its uniqueness, failing to discern that the coming of the Son to be among us makes all things new.

Hebrews will set us straight if we will prayerfully take enough time. Then we will no longer depreciate the old, for we will understand the new in light of the old; and we will no long depreciate the new, for we will see the new in light of the Son, who is the radiance of the divine glory.

■ Applying the Word

Hebrews 1:1-4

1. **As I reflect on my life, what instances come to mind when I sensed that God was speaking to me? What form did this "speaking" take? How willing or unwilling was I to listen and obey what God said?**

2. Many people claim to hear "voices." How can I know that it is God speaking to me and not the devil or even my own secret desires?

3. Hebrews 1:1-4 rings with the majesty and magnificence of Jesus. What other passages in the Bible emphasize Jesus in the same way? How do these passages add to the sense of majesty and awe in Hebrews 1:1-4?

4. How can the message of Hebrews 1:1-4 help me deal with the crime, war, distress, and misery that seem to abound more and more? How, especially, can it help me through the crises in my life?

5. Why is reading from *all* the Bible important? What are the possible consequences of concentrating on one testament? In what ways is Jesus the key to the Old Testament? How does He surpass the Old?

■ Researching the Word

1. Prepare a two-column sheet of paper. Scan the book of Genesis, and in the left column list all the times when God spoke to people. In the right column make a note of *how* God spoke to people. Compare this with what you know from the gospels about how Jesus communicated with people. What contribution does this make to your understanding of Hebrews 1:1, 2?

2. With the aid of a concordance, look up all the references in the New Testament to the word heir. Which ones especially help you to understand the meaning of the word *heir* in Hebrews 1:2? What does the New Testament say about our relationship to God as heirs? In what ways does the Bible suggest that our relationship as heirs is the same and in what ways is it different from Christ's?

3. Look up all the references to *cleanse* and *cleansed* in Hebrews (KJV: purge and purged). Read a few verses before and after each one to get the context. If you have access to the *SDA Bible Commentary*, look up what it says about

purge and *purged* in each of these verses. What do the passages elsewhere in Hebrews add to your understanding of Jesus as He is presented in chapter 1:1-4?

■ Further Study of the Word

1. For a detailed study with reference to the Greek text, see B. F. Westcott, *The Epistle to the Hebrews*, 3-16.
2. For a more general commentary, see F. F. Bruce, *The Epistle to the Hebrews*, rev. ed., 1-9.
3. For an overview of the passage, see W. G. Johnsson, *In Absolute Confidence*, 34-53.

PART TWO

The Magnificence
of Jesus' Person

Hebrews 1:5–7:28

CHAPTER TWO

The Better Name

Hebrews 1:5–2:18

This passage divides into three parts: 1:5-14, where the Son's superiority to angels is established by appeals to Scripture; 2:1-4, the first practical application of the argument; and 2:5-18, a discussion of the Son's human experiences.

Throughout, the person of the Son dominates. He is greater than any angel; to neglect the salvation He has brought entails grave consequences; and the period of the Incarnation—when He became, for a time, lower than the angels—marked merely a temporary change of status.

lower Than angels

Thus, the entire passage elaborates the theme of Hebrews 1:4: "So he became as much superior to the angels as the name he has inherited is superior to theirs." In its development, however, the passage goes much farther. By setting forth the Son as truly divine but also truly man during the Incarnation, it lays the foundation for the major idea of the entire book—Jesus as our High Priest.

■ Getting Into the Word

Hebrews 1:5-14

Read Hebrews 1:5-14 twice. After the second reading, work on the following questions:

1. **How many lines of argument for the Son's superiority to angels do you find? Summarize each of these arguments.**
2. **The notes at the bottom of the page in your NIV Bible**

give you the references for the quotations Paul uses in this section. Look up each in the Old Testament, noting the context. You will find some intriguing information! In order to sharpen the comparative study, draw up a small table with the following items (the first reference is worked as an example):

	Speaker		Person Addressed	
Text	*O.T.*	*Hebrews*	*O.T.*	*Hebrews*
Ps. 2:7	God	God	The king	The Son
2 Sam. 7:14	....	....	....	....

3. What conclusions can you draw from this study about the way the author of Hebrews used the Old Testament? What does it suggest concerning the author's view of the Scripture?
4. What evidence, if any, can you find in this section that the Son isn't merely greater than angels but is truly God?
5. The point of Hebrews 1:5-14 seems clear enough—to show the Son's superiority to angels. Why was this point so important to the apostle? Why did he go to such extended arguments to make sure his readers got the point?

■ Exploring the Word

Behold the Son—How Great He Is!

The apostle immediately picks up the idea of verse 4—the Son's superiority to angels—and begins to prove it. For him, Scripture provides the final word. To clinch the argument there is to rest one's case. And here he finds not just one proof, but a series of passages to establish the Son's magnificence.

All the rest of chapter 1 takes up these proofs from Scripture. We find four main points emerging:

1. Only one Person is ever called "Son" by God (1:5). The author makes the point through a rhetorical question: When he asks, "To which of the angels did God ever say, . . ." the answer understood is "None." No angel ever received this designation. Only Jesus has the better name.
2. Angels worship the Son (1:6). The thought is: The one worshiped is greater than the worshipers; hence, the Son's superiority to angels.
3. The Son is eternal and unchanging, while the angels are created beings (1:7-13). Angels are like the wind or fire. All else grows old and fades away, but the Son is the same for all time.
4. The Son reigns at God's right hand, but angels go out at God's bidding to minister to the saints (1:13, 14). Once again Paul frames the argument in the form of a rhetorical question: "To which of the angels did God ever say . . ." The implied answer is "None."

Behold the Son—how great He is! Greater by reason of name, worship, nature, and service. Look at the Son from any aspect, the apostle is saying, and you'll see how great He is—certainly superior to any angel.

The apostle's stating of his case is clear, but how he brings in Scripture to establish it—that is, his use of the Old Testament quotations—calls for a closer look.

First, we should notice that for every one of the passages quoted, he identifies God as the speaker: "Did God ever say . . ." (1:5); "When God brings his firstborn into the world, he says . . ." (1:6); "But about the Son he says . . ." (1:8); "He also says . . ." (1:10); and, "Did God ever say . . ." (1:13).

Furthermore, in the seven Old Testament texts he cites, four times (1:5, 8, 10, 13) God addresses the Son personally, and in the other three (1:5b, 6, 7), He either speaks about the Son or to angels.

Now let's go back and examine these seven passages in their original context. This comparing of Scripture with Scripture takes some time, but it is the essence of careful Bible study. For only by doing so can we catch the dynamic nature of God's Word and the author's high view of it.

From the footnotes in the New International Version, we learn that Hebrews 1:5 is built on two quotations—Psalm 2:7 and 2 Samuel 7:14. When we turn to these texts in the Old Testament, we find something very interesting—and also very puzzling. Although the words of each citation are identical in both Testaments, and God is the speaker throughout both, the contexts differ markedly.

In its original setting, Psalm 2 describes the enthronement of Israel's king, the Lord's anointed (vss. 1, 6). In verse 7 God goes farther, adopting the monarch as His son and then promising him authority over the nations (verse 8). While Psalm 2 refers to Israel and her kings, the author of Hebrews obviously sees more. He finds here, in leaders like David, a foreshadowing of One far greater—Israel's true King, who alone will fulfill perfectly the description of the psalm.

The second quotation—from 2 Samuel 7:14—jolts us even more. Here we find the prophet Nathan (vs. 4) bringing a message from the Lord to King David. David had proposed to build a temple for Yahweh, but God informs David that He has other plans. Not David, but his son, will construct God's house (vs. 13), and concerning him, the Lord promises, "I will be his father, and he will be my son" (vs. 14).

That is the original setting of the words quoted in the latter half of Hebrews 1:5. God is speaking to David about Solomon. That the promise in its Old Testament context could not refer to Christ becomes sharply clear from the following verse: "When he does wrong, I will punish him with the rod of men, with floggings inflicted by men" (2 Sam. 7:14). That has to be Solomon, not the Messiah!

Once again we see emerging a particular way of understanding the Old Testament. As with Psalm 2, a king of Israel prefigures the King far greater. So the author can select one statement out of a passage—seeing its application to the Son—and bypass a statement that immediately follows in the original passage that could not have Messianic intent.

His third citation (Hebrews 1:6) poses two problems for us. First, although the New International Version footnote refers us to Deuteronomy 32:43, when we turn to that text, we don't find the words quoted in Hebrews—"Let all God's angels worship him." Where is the missing text?

Again the New International Version footnotes give us a clue. The note for Deuteronomy 32:43 tells us that, while the Masoretic text (the version of the Old Testament transmitted for many centuries by the Hebrew scribes) fails to include these words, the Dead Sea Scrolls and the Septuagint (the Old Testament translated into Greek) have something very close: "And let all the angels worship him."

But the context poses a bigger problem. It is, we note, the song of Moses (vs. 1), which he gave to Israel shortly before his death. Throughout this song, and in verse 43, Moses tells about Yahweh, Israel's God. That is, *Moses*, not God, is the speaker. So Paul has taken Moses' statement *about* God and put it in the mouth of God as applying to the Son.

The author's use of the Old Testament here goes beyond what he did with Psalm 2:7 and 2 Samuel 7:14. In those passages we can grasp how Israel's kings could, in a limited fashion, point to the Messiah. But Deuteronomy 32:43 provides no such escape. It seems as if the apostle—under the guidance of the Holy Spirit, we must underline—has used a proof text altogether out of its original context. We will have to return to wrestle with the implications of that undeniable fact when we complete our study of the quotations of Hebrews 1.

Turning to the next citation (Heb. 1:7), we find Psalm 104:4 listed for the source. Problem: When we turn to this passage, we find no mention of angels. The New International Version reads: "He makes winds his *messengers*, flames of fire his servants." However, the Greek may help us out, since the same Greek word (*angelos*) can be translated "angel" or "messenger." We can also assume that the writer of Hebrews quoted this verse from the Septuagint, rather than from the Hebrew text, which would not carry the double meaning.

While we are with Psalm 104, we should observe that the speaker is the psalmist, who is praising God for His mighty acts in nature. That is quite different from Hebrews 1:7, where God is the speaker.

The fifth quotation, Hebrews 1:8, 9, comes without significant change from Psalm 45:6, 7. Once again, however, the speaker in the original context is the psalmist (Ps. 46:1), whereas in Hebrews 1 it is God.

We find a similar use for the next quotation, Hebrews 1:10-12, which quotes (with only minor changes in wording) Psalm 102:25-27. But, as before, there is a transposition in the speaker. In the psalm it is an afflicted person pouring out a lament to God (vss. 1, 24), but in Hebrews 1 the words come from God and are addressed to the Son.

The final citation in the series of proof texts (1:13) again comes without significant change from Psalm 110:1. This psalm is the most quoted part of the Old Testament by new Testament writers, who saw it as pregnant with prophecies of the Messiah. And, of all the many references to the Old Testament that Paul will make in the book of Hebrews, he relies most heavily on this one. We shall see in later chapters how its various predictions will play a critical role in his argument concerning Jesus as heavenly High Priest.

As we review the seven Old Testament quotations in Hebrews 1:5-14, several conclusions suggest themselves. First, the writer used a translation of the Scriptures rather than the original Hebrew for some of his references. Indeed, he was *dependent* on the wording of the translations for two of his arguments (1:6, 7), because the Hebrew text could not have established the points he wished to make.

Second, and more significantly, of the seven quotations, only one—the last—is clearly a Messianic prophecy. Psalm 110 is the only passage we normally would feel free to quote as a prediction of Christ. With all the others we find the author using Scripture in ways that we have been taught to avoid—changing the context, the speaker, or the person addressed.

If we followed his method in writing our term papers and theses, we would be shot down by fellow students and professors! Further, Adventists, along with other Christians who take the Bible seriously, do not employ such an approach to Scripture. We believe and teach that responsible study must always take notice of the context. We have all known people who wrest the Word of God, pulling out a verse here or there to "prove" this pet theory or that. As preachers in training are taught, a text without a context is a pretext.

No wonder students of Hebrews who take time to probe verses 5-14 often come away troubled. But mature reflection yields several insights.

First, we should beware of judging Scripture by our norms of argument and literary analysis. Our era mandates certain rules for using sources. But the Bible comes from a much different age, and the method of reasoning and using Scripture is different also. Not necessarily better or worse—different. Certainly we should beware of an attitude of superiority. Every age thinks its reasoning is the best, but the world moves on, and "time makes ancient good uncouth."

So an idea important to all students of Scripture emerges: Let the Bible explain itself. Don't import our agenda or norms; don't impose our reasoning on the text—let the Word speak to us in its own way. That means we come to the Bible humbly, submissively, ready to listen, ready to learn. The Bible is God's Word to us—it's like no other book and shouldn't be handled like another piece of ancient literature.

That means also that the Bible gives us no license to handle the text irresponsibly, disregarding the context. Paul and other writers were inspired; we are not. So we may not raid the Word, pulling out phrases or verses from their setting in order to claim support for a private theory.

Finally, we come away from Hebrews 1:5-14 profoundly moved at the author's high view of Scripture. For him, Scripture indeed is the Word of God. No matter who the human speaker may be in a particular context, ultimately *God*, not man, is conveying vital truth. This is why he can write in varied situations: "God says . . ."

And, in this exalted understanding of the Old Testament, the Messiah underlies all. Of Him, prophet, priest, and king provide foreshadows; to Him, all God's purposes are moving. To know and acknowledge the Son as truly God, over all and in all, is to see His fingerprints on every page of Scripture.

But Why Such a Long Argument?

Obviously the author wants to establish the deity of the Son of God—that He is exalted high above the angels. We would have thought that a couple of strong texts would be sufficient, for the purpose, but Paul keeps driving home the point, nailing it down by four lines of argument. What he does here is unique in Hebrews. Elsewhere, as we will see, a single passage of Scripture suffices to prove the point.

In trying to figure out why this matter is so important to the author of Hebrews, we search the rest of the book to see whether and how he comes back to this idea. In fact, angels are rarely mentioned elsewhere in this book. The closest to an explanation that we find follows immediately. In chapter 2 angels are mentioned three times, always in a contrasting manner to the Son and His work. Thus, the warning of 2:1-4 comes with greater force to Christians because God's revelation came to them, not through angels, but through the Son. Likewise, God hasn't subjected the age to come to angels but to the Son (vs. 5). And third, Christ in His incarnation didn't take the nature of angels but flesh and blood (vs. 16).

Having granted Paul's use of angels for contrast in chapter 2, the casual nature of their mention doesn't seem to warrant the seriousness of his intent to show the Son's superiority to them in chapter 1:5-14. Surely something else lies back of the development of his argument.

A study of the period just before the birth of Jesus supplies a likely clue. During this time, the Jews gave much attention to angels. They seemed to be fascinated with these heavenly beings, almost obsessed with them. Perhaps the unbending monotheism of Deuteronomy 6:4—"Hear, O Israel . . . the Lord is one"—had made Yahweh seem remote, and the Jews longed for contact with the divine. So angels evoked wonder and admiration: they were the most glorious beings the human mind could imagine. The Jews identified four archangels by name—Michael, Gabriel, Raphael, and Uriel.

In Hebrews 13:8, 9 the apostle warns against strange teachings. Did he have in mind the veneration of angels? Perhaps. We know that Christians in Colossae were dealing in angel worship (Col. 2:18). We also know from the nonbiblical literature of the time that Jewish speculation about angels sometimes had angels engaging in ministry in a heavenly temple. Even Melchizedek emerges. A scroll from Qumran, though poorly preserved, assigns him a role of heavenly mediation.

With such interest prevailing, we can see why it would be vital to establish at the outset of Hebrews the superiority of the Son. As great as any angel might be, Jesus is infinitely superior. He, the eternal, unchanging One, is the object of angel worship and service, for He is God!

■ Getting Into the Word

Hebrews 2

Read Hebrews 2 twice. On the second reading, begin to look for answers to the following items:

1. **Find 2:1 in different versions. Do you notice any major differences in the translation?**
2. **How does the seriousness of Christian life come through in 2:1-4?**
3. **In this chapter we can see the experiences of the Son in terms of a V- or U-shaped curve that starts with His life**

before the Incarnation, covers the Incarnation, and then goes beyond. Draw such a V- or U-curve, noting significant points on it.

4. In contrast with chapter 1, which strongly affirms the true deity of the Son, chapter 2 affirms His true humanity. List all the evidences you can find in this chapter that show this vital truth.

5. Make a list of what Jesus accomplished by becoming human.

6. Study the quotation used at 2:6-8, paying special attention to its original meaning. Now study it in paragraph 2:5-9. What point is the author of Hebrews bringing out by means of this passage?

7. Look up in a concordance references to Jesus' suffering in Hebrews. What did His suffering entail?

8. What does 2:10 mean—Jesus being made "perfect"? Look up other references to His perfecting in Hebrews, and try to reach a conclusion.

9. Look at the three quotations employed in 2:12, 13, noting the Old Testament context, speaker, and person(s) addressed. Does our study of 1:5-14 help you understand how Paul uses Scripture here?

10. Hebrews 2 is one of the strongest statements of Jesus' genuine humanity in all the Bible, yet it comes right after the powerful affirmation of His deity in chapter 1. To get the contrast of these two fundamental ideas placed back to back, read 1:1–2:18 in a single sitting. Do you find any explanation as to *how* deity and humanity can be blended in the one Person?

11. We find Jesus as High Priest first mentioned in Hebrews 2:17. What other references to these words or to the idea can you find in the New Testament outside the book of Hebrews?

12. In chapter 2, what verse or verses leave the strongest impression with you, speaking to your heart and nurturing your spiritual life?

■ Exploring the Word

Our Faith Is Precious—Take It Seriously

The second chapter of Hebrews flows on from the first, with the discussion moving forward clearly and logically. We need to remember that the chapter and verse divisions, so familiar to us, didn't come from the writer. They were added many centuries later. These divisions help us in separating smaller and larger units of thought (although occasionally the breaks have been poorly placed) and in enabling us to make reference to Scripture. But we shouldn't let them dictate our understanding.

So this is what we find in Hebrews: a magnificently charted course of argument that rolls on like a river rising in the mountains and journeying steadily toward the ocean. In this book, above all others of the Bible, we need to start at the beginning—in the mountains—and let the book explain itself. To jump into the discussion somewhere along the way is to invite misunderstanding.

The first four verses of Hebrews 2 illustrate the point. They arise directly out of the ideas developed in chapter 1—the magnificence of the Son as fully, eternally God. We find the "therefore" of 2:1 taking these conceptions and applying them directly and personally. Chapter 1 tells us the "What," chapter 2:1-4 the "so what." If the ideas of chapter 1 are correct, *then* this is what they mean to us.

This break in the argument—the first of several we will find in the book—comes as a word of warning. The first readers—and we!—must be vigilant, lest we not only take lightly our faith but fall into judgment because of neglecting that which is so precious.

Paul highlights our specific danger in two phrases: "Drift[ing] away" from what we have heard (2:1) and ignoring "such a great salvation" (2:3).

Some translations give a different rendering for verse 1. For example, the Kings James Version says, "Lest at any time we should let them *slip*." This is because the same Greek verb *pararreō* can be used for a ship that drifts off course or for a ring that slips off the finger. While the two images are vastly different, the point is quite clear—the loss of something important.

Even though we have started out on course, the winds and the currents may pull us far out of line, and yet we won't even be aware of it! Or, changing the metaphor, the ring slips from the finger while we are busy with the affairs of life. Caught up in our activities, we have lost it—and don't realize it!

How can we avoid such loss? By paying "more careful attention . . . to what we have heard" (2:1). That is, by keeping alert and diligent, checking to see that we're still on course, that we haven't lost what we should safeguard as precious.

Relationships aren't self-perpetuating. We have to work to keep them fresh. A relationship that isn't growing closer is beginning to wither. As soon as we begin to take for granted a friend of many years, we begin to lose that friend. Husbands and wives who start life together blissfully happy and in love, who struggle through years of making a home and raising children and winning financial security, wonder why their love for each other dies after twenty, thirty, or forty years. What happened? Where did love go? Chances are that nothing happened to make love leave—what *didn't* happen brought on the problem. As soon as the couple pride themselves on the good marriage they have and begin coasting, they're heading for disaster.

So with our faith. Jesus is precious, as is the salvation He has brought us. No matter how much we love Him, how fervent our desire for Him, that relationship must be continually renewed. Day by day we must seek to know Him better, to love Him more truly, to serve Him more faithfully. The alternative is drifting—with shipwreck on the shoals of neglect.

In 2:3 the apostle goes one step farther. Ignoring God's most valued gift—Jesus and His salvation—exposes us to judgment. He gives us a warning from God's people in Old Testament times: When they disobeyed the divine message mediated through angels, they suffered punishment. The reference probably is to the giving of God's law at Sinai: Acts 7:53 and Galatians 3:19 tell us that this revelation was "put into effect through angels."

Paul reasons from the lesser to the greater in Hebrews 2:2, 3. If the ancient Israelites came under divine judgment when they violated the message spoken *by angels*, how should we expect to escape judgment if we ignore the message spoken *by the Lord?* Obviously, we cannot. Our sin is greater than theirs.

In the last part of verse 3 and in verse 4, Paul lists items that make the message from the Lord (Jesus and His salvation) so great. First, it came from the Lord Himself, not any angel—and chapter 1 already established the Lord's superiority to angels. Second, the message was confirmed by "those who heard Him"—the apostolic witnesses, those who had been with Jesus throughout His ministry, seeing His mighty acts, hearing His teachings. Third, God testified to the divine credentials of the message. Miracles and gifts of the Holy Spirit—the book of Acts tells the story—showed heaven's blessing on the new Christian faith.

Jesus, the apostolic witness, the gifts—all showed that something new and extraordinary had happened. All pointed to the most wonderful event in the history of humanity—to God's coming to us so that we might have access to His most precious gifts.

If we ignore *that*, how can we escape! We deserve whatever God has reserved for those who don't want what He graciously provided.

But here's the point of Hebrews 2:1-4 (and we shall meet it again in the book): Our danger as Christians isn't so much an outright spurning of salvation so great. Our danger is that, having begun well and right on course, we will drift off course. Although we're bound for the Promised Land, we're still very much on earth, and the values of life right here and now can dull our spiritual desires and perceptions.

Frankly, that's what I see happening in the church today. We take our precious Lord and His love for granted. We don't *value* membership in His body, the church. We take it much less seriously than Rotarians, who would lose their membership in their club if they skipped meetings. We're in grave danger of drifting off course, ignoring our magnificent Lord and His salvation.

No matter who we are or what position we have in the church, *relationship always growing*

from janitor to General Conference president, we face the danger outlined in Hebrews 2:1-4. But the safeguard can also be ours: to pay "more careful attention . . . to what we have heard." That means keeping alert, keeping faith fresh and strong and growing, keeping our relationship with the Lord young. It means continually reminding ourselves who Jesus is—how magnificent is His person. We must also remind ourselves about His gift of eternal life to us—how magnificent are His saving death and saving heavenly ministry.

That's why the book of Hebrews speaks so powerfully to us in these last days. When we let its truths about Jesus—His person and His work—wash over our souls, when we grasp them and receive them not only intellectually but in the heart, when we weep and wonder at the suffering of the Son, we will not—we cannot—let these ideas slip away.

The Son's Career—From the Highest to the Lowest

To the reasoning of chapter 1 that shows the Son exalted far above the angels, those enamored of these heavenly beings might well have replied, "Higher than angels? No way—He died on a cross!" Hebrews 2 will answer this objection, taking the offensive as well as defending against this point. The author will argue that the Son's inferiority to angels was only a *temporary* matter; but further, that God willed it so that the Son might accomplish achievements possible in no other way.

Hebrews 2:5-9 summarizes the varied stages of the Son's career. From the lofty status of chapter 1:5-14, where angels worship and serve Him, we see a dramatic change—He becomes lower than the angels. God has become man! And not only become man, but the God-man suffers death!

However, the career continues. After this incredible condescension, the Son is restored to glory and honor. Not in spite of His incarnation and death, but *because* of it! His death isn't counted a failure but a triumph and victory. The Son's career thus follows a V shape:

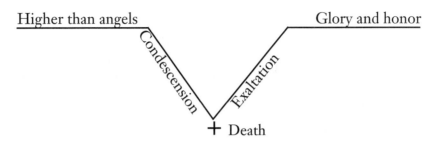

Higher than angels   Glory and honor

Condescension   *Exaltation*

✝ Death

These five verses are loaded with interesting insights. First, we notice the quotation from Psalm 8:4-6 that introduces the discussion. That psalm in its original context sings the glory of humanity, created by God to have dominion over the world. In status, that humanity is only a little lower than the angels.

Commentators are divided over the function of this quotation in Hebrews. Many see it describing God's original plan for humanity, the divine ideal. But because of the Fall, we haven't lived up to that goal—none except Jesus. He is the perfect Man, in whom God's purpose for the race at last comes to fruition.

As attractive as I find that interpretation, I don't think it rings true to the context. We should seek for the function of the quotation, not in its own words, but in the manner in which the author applies the words. And verse 9 shows clearly what is his point: not in man, per se, but in the V-shaped career of the Son. Further, this concentration on the Son in His human experiences will be elaborated through the remainder of the chapter. The Son, not humanity, forms the focus of interest.

Psalm 8, therefore, functions as a prediction of the Son's career. He is the Son of Man who would become lower than the angels, but who subsequently would be exalted far above them. So the writer of Hebrews has a powerful answer for Christians intoxicated with the veneration of angels who were discouraged by the Son's human experiences. Scripture actually predicted His career! No mistake, no aberration here—search the Scriptures, and you will find that this was what God intended.

Note the reference to "a little lower" in verse 7. The footnote says, "For a little while" lower. This is accurate to the Greek text, which puts two diminutives together—literally, "a little little." These diminutives can refer to either status or time, so "a little while" lower is an altogether acceptable understanding. And that is precisely the point of verse 9—Jesus, who *became* lower than the angels, did not *remain* lower, for after His death He was crowned with glory and honor.

The most important point in Paul's argument goes beyond such niceties of Greek grammar, however. As he describes the career of the Son, his thought gravitates to its key moment, the event that was at once its low point and paradoxically its greatest. Calvary! Jesus' death made all the difference.

All New Testament thought centers in Calvary. All four Gospel writers shape their lives of Jesus around His death. In many respects the Gospels are stories of the Passion, with the chapters leading up to Jesus' final week as the introduction. All the apostolic preaching in Acts centers in Calvary. All the letters of the New Testament, and the Apocalypse as well, take Calvary as their immovable anchor point. For this is the gospel that "I passed on to you as of first importance; that Christ died for our sins according to the Scriptures" (1 Cor. 15:3).

New Testament Christians never fail to give Calvary prime time. Although Jesus' death on a cross scandalized the Jews (a suffering Messiah) and made merry the Greek (an executed felon), Christians weren't ashamed. They didn't try to hide the cross or excuse the cross; they weren't embarrassed by it. To the world around them, Calvary was the worst way to die—a death so humiliating that by law, no Roman citizen could be subject to it. To Christians, Calvary was God's way of reconciling the world to Himself. Not a failure, but a resounding victory! Not a tragic end, but the salvation of humanity!

And that is just what Hebrews 2:9 affirms: Jesus was crowned with glory and honor *because* He suffered death.

Two expressions of verse 9 especially demand our attention. Paul tells us that Jesus "*taste[d]* death for everyone." The famous preacher Chrysostom, from the early church, interpreted these words to mean that Jesus experienced just enough of death's bitterness to know what it is like. He likened Jesus to a physician who, in order to encourage his patient to swallow the medicine, puts the bitter potion to his own lips and sips a little.

As great a preacher as Chrysostom was, he badly misconstrued this text. Jesus didn't merely sip the cup of death—He drank it to the dregs. *Tasting* tells us that He *really* died, *really* experienced death. See Jesus in the Garden of Gethsemane as He shrinks from the rejection, spitting, and flogging that lie just ahead and especially from the God-forsakenness of Calvary. See Him agonizing in prayer, pleading for another way. Hear His plaintive cry, thrice given: " 'My Father, if it is possible, may this cup be taken from me. Yet not as I will, but as you will' " (Matt. 26:39). But it wasn't possible—not if He was to win the world back to God. And so He went to the cross, dying alone, dying for everyone. He tasted death—not just physical death, but the horror of separation from God, which the Bible calls "the second death" (Rev. 20:6).

Hebrews 2:9 also tells us that Jesus tasted death "by the grace of God." The majority of ancient manuscripts read this way, but a few of the very earliest have a startling variant: "apart from God." The change involves just two letters of the Greek alphabet. Obviously, someone, probably in the second century, changed a couple of letters in copying the book of Hebrews—but in which direction was the change made?

In my judgment, the minority case seems the more likely. I think those few very old manuscripts probably are correct, that the original text of Hebrews set out the death of Jesus in the starkest terms. I see Jesus' dying "apart from God" as a direct echo of that terrible moan from the cross, " 'My God, my God, why have you forsaken me?' " (Matt. 27:46). I see it alluded to again in Hebrews 5:7, where the author vividly portrays the prayers, petitions, loud cries, and tears of Jesus as He went forward to death.

Whatever reading we choose to accept for this phrase in 2:9, the overall idea is abundantly clear. Jesus' death was terribly, fiercely, gut-wrenchingly real. There is no make-believe here, no play acting. It is the lowest point in human experience, and for the Son, the lowest of the lowest.

But I repeat it, at the risk of offending: This frank acknowledgment of what Calvary meant, this honest appraisal, wasn't something for Christians to be ashamed of. Jesus' death—this lowest of the lowest—was His greatest achievement. *Because* He went so low, He could be exalted so high; and *because* He tasted death, everyone—that means me—can have eternal life.

As we reflect on the magnificent concepts of Hebrews 2:7-9, two impressions burn themselves into our minds. First, what a God! Not one who remains passive and unmoved like the gods of the Greeks, but a God who changes, entering into time and space to win our salvation. He takes our problems on Himself, becoming one with us, in order to deliver us. What a God! He descends and condescends, humiliating Himself in service to win the world.

But how can these things be? How can God become man? Does the God-man have one mind or two (divine and human), one will or two? If He is truly God, can He be truly man?

With such questions Christians have struggled since the dawn of our faith. The author of Hebrews provides no answers—not even a hint. We find affirmation, not explanation. As chapter 1 sets out the deity of the Son in uncompromising terms, so chapter 2 asserts His full, undiluted humanity. The *fact* of Jesus, Son of God and Son of man, is for our contemplation and adoration, not our mental gymnastics.

The remainder of Hebrews 1 further elaborates the two leading thoughts of verses 7 to 9: the reality of Jesus' humanity and what He accomplished by the Incarnation.

Truly Human—One With Us

Paul argues the true humanity of Jesus in two ways—nature and experiences. That is, Jesus became part of the human family, (nature), and He passed through the same sort of life events that we all encounter.(experiences).

Verse 11 tells us that He and we "are of the same family." The Greek for this expression is literally "all of one"—of one origin or of one nature. In this verse the "one who makes men holy" refers to Jesus, and we are "those who are made holy." The marvelous idea coming through is that Jesus, who sets us apart for Himself and transforms us into His likeness, is *one of us*. He is, as verse 10 says, the author (or captain, pioneer, pathfinder) of our salvation. He has been over the way ahead of us, blazed the trail, charted the course. He knows and understands what it is like to be human. Christianity is "all in the family"!

This leads to His recognition of us as His siblings. Although we are a ragtag bunch of wandering sheep who have disgraced the family's good name, He identifies Himself with us. He isn't ashamed to be counted in the same family with us!

Throughout human history, sons or daughters who go astray and embarrass the family find themselves, like Cain—out on the edge. In earlier generations they simply went or were sent out of sight and out of mind to "the colonies." Today they merge with the crowds in some large city, forgotten, rarely mentioned in polite circles. Then there are the unfortunate family members, those born with defective minds or bodies. In the past these unfortunate people were put away in a charitable home or kept out of sight. They bore the family's name, but the family, ashamed, sought to hide them.

But Jesus comes to us and says, "My brothers!" "My sisters!" Rascals, wastrels though we are, disgracing the Father's good name, He seeks us out and identifies with us. Broken and feeble in body or in mind though we may be, He doesn't turn red with embarrassment over us. He welcomes us into His family.

The three quotations in Hebrews 2:12, 13, taken from Psalm 22:22 and Isaiah 8:17, 18, all reinforce this point of kinship. Although the Old Testament contexts were considerably different— the speaker in the psalm being David, and Isaiah 8:17, 18 referring to the prophet and his sons—the author of Hebrews sees in these words apt descriptions of Jesus' relation to us. Our discussion of the use of the Old Testament in 1:5-14 helps us understand the way the writer calls upon Scripture to support key points of his argument.

The affirmation of Jesus' genuine humanity continues in 2:14.

Although the Son is fully, eternally God, He took flesh and blood. He didn't merely take the *appearance*, but not the reality, of our nature (as some Christians concluded who wrestled with the mystery of the Incarnation). No! He took our very nature.

Nor did He stoop to become an angel. He went much lower—to Abraham's descendants. He became "like his brothers in every way" (vs. 7). Hebrews 2 specifies no exception to Jesus' identification with us, but 4:15 introduces a vital qualification—"yet was without sin." That point will demand important elaboration when Jesus' high-priestly ministry comes under review.

Of the same family, brother, flesh and blood, like us in every way—the true humanity of Jesus cannot be denied. And to cap the point, He shares our experiences as He shares our nature: He suffers, is tempted, even dies.

Jesus' suffering is mentioned in six places in Hebrews (2:9, 10, 18; 5:7, 8; 9:26; 13:12). In almost every case, the discussion focuses on His death. So the writer isn't addressing the general problem of human woe—our heartaches, sicknesses, tragedies, and grief.

While Jesus did identify with these experiences, the concern in Hebrews runs along spiritual lines. Jesus' suffering here focuses on the agony with which He went to His death—and so accomplished the divine will.

Likewise, Jesus was tested or tempted (2:18; again in 4:15—"tempted in every way, just as we are"). He could have yielded to Satan, could have fallen. In coming to earth in true humanity, He "risk[ed] . . . failure and eternal loss" (White, *The Desire of Ages,* 49). In my judgment, one of the sharpest distortions of the Gospels is the theology (even though it has centuries of tradition behind it) that denies the possibility of Jesus' sinning because He was God.

This, after all, is what Jesus' becoming part of our family must mean—vulnerability. He will share our openness to temptation, our risk, our vulnerability. Choice will be real for Him, as it is for us. Anything less, and His humanity collapses into sham, no matter what theological phrases we may heap upon it.

Jesus' temptations and ours: Are they identical? No, just as no two people today have identical temptations. We each come to the moment of testing with our own bag of inherited strengths, weaknesses, and life choices ready-made that predispose us either to resist or to fall. Nor do any two moments of testing equate: Each has its milieu of circumstances, its particular and peculiar allurements.

But the essence of all temptations remains the same, across culture and across time: "The cravings of sinful man, the lust of his eyes and the boasting of what he has and does" (1 John 2:16). For Jesus, as for us, the "bottom line" is the Father's will: "Will we obey it, or will we follow our own? So although Jesus didn't live with liquor stores and movies and Wall Street, He faced what we all face: the moment of testing when the devil offers us a shortcut across God's plan for us.

Jesus' human experience reaches a climax in an expression used by the author of Hebrews that at first glance seems incredible— His being "made perfect." We find the expression used in two places besides 2:10 (5:9; 7:28), so it isn't a puzzling aside. In trying to understand what Paul means by this term, we can quickly set aside two answers that some have suggested.

He doesn't mean that Jesus was *raised* to a divine status that He didn't previously have (what theologians call an "adoptionistic Christology"). The reasoning of chapter 1 clearly eliminates this possibility. Nor does Paul mean that the Son had a sin problem that He had to overcome, some moral imperfection to be purified by His own suffering. Hebrews declares unequivocally the sinlessness of the Son (4:15; 7:26-28).

Rather, Jesus' being "made perfect" describes His maturing, His ongoing experiences—culminating in the suffering of the cross—that prepared Him for the divine work. By passing through our human experiences, He became qualified, or equipped, for the role God had laid out for Him.

With this conclusion, we are ready to summarize what Jesus accomplished by His humanity.

From Here to Eternity: All We Ever Needed

Jesus delivered us from bondage in this life, saved us from eternal death, and qualified Himself to become our great High Priest—and all because of, and only because of, the Incarnation. That is, all we need now and forever He made possible by becoming one with us.

Of these three achievements, His saving work on the cross must be given first place. In 2:9, when the author sketches the V-shaped career of the Son, His death stands out as the critical moment. *Because* of His death, He now is crowned with glory and honor; He tasted death for everyone.

The statement oft made by Christians is true: This baby was born to die. We dimly comprehend the plan of redemption, but the Bible makes one fact crystal clear: Only by Christ's dying could we be delivered from our burden of guilt, shame, and death. Christ did not die as a martyr but as the Saviour of the world.

He died *for* (on behalf of) everyone. He died in my place; when He died, *I* died. "Christ was treated as we deserve, that we might be treated as He deserves. He was condemned for our sins, in which he had no share, that we might be justified by His righteousness, in which we had no share. He suffered the death which was ours, that we might receive the life which was His. 'With His stripes we are healed' " (White, *The Desire of Ages*, 25).

In 2:10, the author of Hebrews makes a statement quite unlike any other found in all Scripture. He tells us that it was "fitting" for God to make Jesus perfect through suffering, as though Paul is passing judgment on the propriety of what God did. This reasoning surprises us, for throughout the Bible, God does what He does, with or without humanity's approval. God is God and not man. Who are we to say what befits Him?

Today we often hear people commenting about God, usually in negative terms. They think God is unfair, cruel, or capricious. They venture to suggest what God should or should not do. But, as F. F. Bruce notes, such comments tell us not a whit about God—only about the persons making the observations (Bruce, *The Epistle to the Hebrews*, rev. ed., 79).

Yet here in Hebrews 2:10 we read that it "befitted" God to lead Jesus through human experiences that culminated in the suffering of Calvary. Paul's point is surely what we noticed above—that only through His becoming human and dying our death could the Son accomplish the divine plan for our eternal salvation.

But Jesus did more than save us from eternal death. He delivered us from the bondage of the *fear* of death. In 2:14, 15 we catch the poignant note of human helplessness before the ancient enemy. "Our sweetest songs are those that tell of saddest thought," wrote the poet Shelley, and the saddest thoughts always come back to death, no matter what the century. Whether in ancient Rome at the loss of a friend, whether twentieth-century Kafka or Sartre or Hemingway reflecting on the meaninglessness of human existence ("a dirty joke") in the face of the grim reaper's inevitability, the melody is the same—plaintive and infinitely sad. Humanity is in bondage to the fear of death.

But not for believers in Jesus!

The eternal Son has become a man, has entered death's dark cavern, and has disarmed its jailer. By consenting to death, He has destroyed death itself. So for us who believe in Him, death already has lost its sting. Although we mourn our dear ones who pass from this life, we sorrow not as others, who have no hope. For us, every sunrise doesn't arrive tinged with pain because we know that night must follow; for us, every dawning comes bright with the promise of Him who put death to flight. Life is beautiful. We could wish summer's warmth to last forever. But as we sense the nights grow long and feel the catch in our breath, we know that when the long journey comes, we will be safe in the hands of Him who is the Resurrection and the Life.

Jesus—now and forever. Jesus, in this life and the next—and, says Hebrews, for all that lies between.

For not only did He win our ransom from eternal death by tasting the death that was ours; not only did He shatter death's bonds for our life here and now—He has qualified as our great *High Priest*. He became like us, His family members, in every respect—tempted, suffering, maturing, dying. Only thus could He become a merciful and faithful High Priest.

This verse, 2:17, is the first place we find Jesus called High Priest in Hebrews. Indeed, it is the first place in all the Bible where we find it. The manner in which the term occurs, however—casually, without explanation—suggests that the idea was already familiar to the readers. And, indeed, while Jesus isn't specifically *called* High Priest in any book of Scripture apart from Hebrews, He is *portrayed* as High Priest in several other places. For instance, in Romans 8:34—He is "at the right hand of God and is also interceding for us." In Revelation He is dressed as a priest (1:13) and also appears as the sacrificial Lamb (5:6).

Jesus as our heavenly High Priest—in His person and work—forms the summit of the theological development of Hebrews. We shall look at His priesthood closely in later chapters. Suffice it here to notice the point made by the author in 2:17—Jesus *became* High Priest. Only because He became human and passed through human experiences did He qualify to be our great High Priest.

Indeed, the arguments of 1:5-14 (Jesus as truly God) and of 2:5-18 (Jesus as truly Man) intersect at 2:17. He, the God-Man, touches both deity and humanity, and thereby becomes High Priest.

■ Applying the Word

Hebrews 1:5–2:18

1. In view of the magnificent ideas presented in Hebrews 1:5–2:18, what is my response to Jesus?
2. What earthly "angels" or "stars" tend to attract my admiration and imitation? How does Jesus, the Superstar of all existence, differ from these?
3. How could I use Hebrews 1 to give a Bible study about Jesus as truly God?
4. What does the great salvation that I have through Jesus mean to me? As I review my spiritual experience, am I on

course or drifting? In what ways am I closer to God than I was a year ago? Than when I first accepted Christ as Saviour?

5. Reflect on the following advice by Ellen White: "It would be well for us to spend a thoughtful hour each day in contemplation of the life of Christ. We should take it point by point, and let the imagination grasp each scene, especially the closing ones. As we thus dwell upon His great sacrifice for us, our confidence in Him will be more constant, our love will be quickened, and we shall be more deeply imbued with His spirit. If we would be saved at last, we must learn the lesson of penitence and humiliation at the foot of the cross" (White, *The Desire of Ages*, 83). What benefits can I expect to gain from meditating on Christ's life in this way? Am I practicing that counsel?

6. What does it mean to me that Jesus regards Himself as my Brother?

7. Am I afraid to die? How can the liberating power of Jesus, the Conqueror of death, set me free from the fear of death?

8. What does it mean to turn to Jesus for help to overcome?

9. Which verse in Hebrews 1:5–2:18 impresses me most? Why?

■ Researching the Word

1. With the help of a concordance, study the references to the death of Jesus in the New Testament. Study also Isaiah 53. Make a list of all that Jesus accomplished by His death. What new insights have you gained from this study about the meaning of Christ's death for you personally.

2. In Hebrews 1:5-14 Paul emphasizes the deity of Christ. Do a study of the deity of Christ in the Bible.
   a. Read the first section under the heading "Jesus Christ" in the *SDA Bible Dictionary* (585), and look up all the references given there for the divinity of Christ. Also look up John 1:1-3 and Colossians 1:15-17.

    b. Look up John 8:58 in a Bible that has marginal references, and follow through the cross-references to other occurrences of the expression "I am" in the Gospels, especially John.

    c. Read Exodus 3, where the name "I am" first appears in the Bible. Compare verses 2 and 14. What difference do you notice between who each verse said appeared to Moses? How do you reconcile Exodus 3:2 with Hebrews 1:1-14?

    d. Read the article "The Names of God in the Old Testament" in the *SDA Bible Commentary*, 1:170-173.

    e. What difference does the knowledge of Christ's divinity make to your Christian experience? How would it affect your Christian experience if you did not believe in His divinity?

■ Further Study of the Word

1. For more information on the way the author quotes Old Testament Scripture, see F. F. Bruce, *The Epistle to the Hebrews*, 25-29.
2. For a discussion about Jesus as our Brother, see W. G. Johnsson, *In Absolute Confidence*, 54-74.
3. For a careful, detailed commentary on Hebrews 2, see B. F. Westcott, *The Epistle to the Hebrews*, 36-71.
4. For an inspiring description of Jesus as truly God and truly Man, see Ellen G. White, *The Desire of Ages*, 19-26.

CHAPTER THREE

The Better
Leader

Hebrews 3:1–4:13

The apostle's development in chapters 1 and 2 reached a climax at 2:17, where Christ becomes a merciful and faithful High Priest. Over the course of the next four chapters, he takes up, in turn, these twin characteristics of mercifulness and faithfulness, but in reverse order. In 3:1–4:13 he emphasizes Jesus' faithfulness, and in 4:14–6:20 His mercy. Of the two, mercy emerges the more prominently.

Hebrews 3:1–4:13 itself falls into three distinct parts. In 3:1-6a Paul compares and contrasts Jesus and Moses; 3:6b-19 sounds a warning from Israel's failure of old; and 4:1-13 comes with an invitation for the Hebrew Christians to press on resolutely to the promised goal.

■ Getting Into the Word

Hebrews 3:1-19

Read Hebrews 3:1–4:13, noting the three parts to the discussion and trying to see how each flows into the next. Then read chapter 3 again, carefully and prayerfully. Here are some questions to stimulate your study:

1. What words or ideas bind together the three parts of 3:1–4:13?
2. Why is Jesus called an "apostle" in 3:1? Does this term come up again in Hebrews? Can you find other places in

the New Testament where this designation is used of
Him? (Use a concordance.)

3. Moses is the foremost leader of God's people in the Old
   Testament. On the basis of 3:1-6a, draw up a list comparing and contrasting Moses and Jesus.

4. Where else do we find Moses mentioned in Hebrews?
   Would you say that Moses plays a prominent role in this
   book?

5. What is the "house" referred to in 3:1-6a?

6. Upon which Old Testament passage does the writer draw
   in 3:6b-19? Go back and read this passage in its context.

7. Study the way the apostle uses *today*. Note that it comes
   up again in 4:7. Is *today* a time of warning or of invitation?

8. Why did Israel of old fail? Was their leader defective?
   What happened to their motivation?

9. Notice the word *rest* in 3:1-19. It figures prominently in
   4:1-13 also, but confine your study to chapter 3 for now.
   On the basis of 3:6b-19, what does *rest* seem to mean?

10. As you review the application of 3:6b-19, compare it with
    the first one (2:1-3). Wherein does this second one build
    on the first and amplify it?

■ Exploring the Word

One word, in several different forms, ties together the three
sections of 3:1–4:13, but our English translations make it hard for
us to see the linkage. Thus it is time for a little Greek study so we
can see how the author's thought is running. The key word is
pistis, which means "faith." Here are the various forms in which it
appears in this part of Hebrews:

pistis	=	faith
pistos	=	faithful
pisteuō	=	to have faith
apistia	=	absence of faith ("unfaith")

Unfortunately, English translations introduce *belief* into the discussion. However, there is no separate word for *belief* in the Greek. The English language distinguishes between faith and belief, but the Greek has one and the same word, *pistis*. The same holds for the verb *pisteuō* and the word for absence of faith—*apistia*. The use of *believe* and *unbelief* confuses the argument and makes it difficult for us to see how the one idea runs throughout 3:1–4:13.

In 3:1-6a Paul emphasizes Jesus as the *faithful* (*pistos*) leader. In 3:6b-19 he shows how the Israelites of old failed because of their *lack of faith* (*apistia*). And his reasoning in 4:1-13 binds up the discussion by calling his Christian readers to *faith* (pistis).

The Faithful Leader

The chapter begins with an invitation to "fix your thoughts" on Jesus. Toward the end of the sermon, at 12:1-3, Paul makes a similar appeal. Just what is he calling us to do?

For some Christians, talk about Jesus focuses on theological questions and arguments. They seek to probe the mysteries of the Word made flesh. They seek to understand how this one Individual could be at once truly God and truly human. They explore the intricacies of His human nature—was it just like ours? Was it like Adam's before the Fall or after the Fall?

Now, such inquiry is important. Jesus Christ stands at the center of the Christian faith, with His own words challenging every person: "Who do *you* say I am?" (Matt. 16:15). Everything depends on the answer we give. To acknowledge Him as truly God and yet truly human, as the Scriptures teach, means to accept His claims to be Saviour and Lord.

So discussions and disagreements about Jesus aren't necessarily bad. We must have a solid doctrinal basis for taking issue with those such as the Jehovah's Witnesses, who deny His eternal deity, or with those who would deny that He could have sinned.

However, Jesus is unique. In seeking to understand Him, we are probing God, so our comprehension inevitably falls short. We do well, as Ellen White suggested, to take off our shoes, for we walk on holy ground (*The Youth's Instructor*, 13 Oct. 1898). We should beware of going beyond Scripture. For instance, from a purely logical point of view, Jesus could not have been both fully divine and fully human. Thus the tendency is to emphasize one side and negate or weaken the other. But then we fall into error.

Hebrews, in its call to "fix our thoughts" on Jesus, does not encourage such speculation. Nor does it primarily suggest that we contemplate Jesus as an example of Christian conduct, whose victory provides a model for us. No, the discussion of Jesus' person and work in chapter 2 and throughout the book leads in a different direction. We are to trust what Jesus has done rather than try to do what He has done.

So in 3:1, the writer ties consideration of Jesus to His role as Apostle and High Priest. As the popular song of faith tells us, we are to turn our eyes upon Jesus and away from the world, contemplating the victory He has won.

Jesus as High Priest forms the major motif of Hebrews, and we shall study it closely in subsequent chapters. But what about Jesus as Apostle? This is the only place we find such a designation in the entire New Testament. The word itself means "one who is sent," suggesting a *mission* interest. And that is just what Hebrews 1 and 2 have portrayed: the Son's preexistence, the break in His exalted state when He became man and lower than angels, and His exaltation—"crowned with glory and honor"—following the Cross. Jesus was the divine Messenger, One sent from heaven to win our salvation. He was God's Apostle.

Although only here does Scripture call Jesus "apostle," the idea occurs throughout the New Testament. The Gospel of John, in particular, frequently sets forth Jesus as the One sent by the Father. For example: "As the Father has sent me, I am sending you" (John 20:21).

In 3:1, therefore, *apostle* sums up what has gone before, and *high priest* gathers together the exciting theological plan that is to come.

First, we find a discussion of the faithfulness of Jesus, our High Priest. Paul makes the point by comparing and contrasting Jesus and Moses—the latter, the outstanding leader of the Old Testament; the former, the supreme figure of the New Testament.

These leaders of God's people have one outstanding trait in common—they are faithful to God. But Jesus is greater for three reasons:

Jesus	**Moses**
1. Son.	1. Servant.
2. Builder of "the house" (over "the house").	2. Part of "the house" (in "the house").
3. Fulfillment of Old Testament revelation.	3. Witness to revelation to come.

In these verses, 3:2-6a, we see two periods of history side by side—the Exodus and the new exodus under Christ. We see Moses, an outstanding figure who discharged his duties unswervingly. But we see the One far greater, of whom Moses was a type and to whom he testified.

Moses will surface again in the argumentation of Hebrews. We find him among the heroes of faith (11:23-29) and also in a striking passage in 12:18-24. However, Moses does not play a major role in the theological development of Hebrews. He stands primarily as a representative of the old system of sanctuary and sacrifice—given at Sinai—and Hebrews will continually highlight the superiority of the new.

The references to *house* in 3:2-6a take us back to Numbers 12:7, where God said of Moses, "He is faithful in all my house." *House* refers to the community of God's people, whether at the time of Moses or in the Christian era.

We can count on Jesus—that is the point of 3:1-6a. If Moses led God's people with integrity and devotion to the task, how much more our Leader! We *know* we have a faithful High Priest in Jesus, not only because of affirming statements but also because He demonstrated unswerving integrity in His human experiences. Tempted, tested, suffering, dying, He never yielded, never fell, never turned back. So He became our faithful High Priest.

Faithfulness—Christian assurance depends on it. Someone we can trust. Someone in whom we can have absolute confidence. Someone who will never let us down. Someone who is the same yesterday, today, and forever (13:8).

Jesus, our faithful High Priest.

Lessons From Israel's Unfaithfulness

With the "if" of 3:6b, the author brings us back to application. Membership in God's house isn't automatic or independent of human effort. We must "hold on." We must endure. To start is good, but to arrive is the goal.

The long application will take us through two steps. In 3:7-19 we see a negative example—the tribes of Israel who started out from Egypt but who failed to make it through to the Promised Land. We will see why they fell short and what lessons their failure holds for Christians today. In 4:1-13, the exhortation turns from warning to invitation. Here the experience of Israel fades from view as the apostle holds out to his readers God's promises and purpose.

In drawing attention to Israel's experience, Paul doesn't turn back to the Pentateuch (the first five books of the Bible) for a scriptural basis. Instead, he goes to his preferred source for Old Testament meditation—the Psalms—and selects a passage that provides rich material for his appeal. Psalm 95:7-11 not only summarizes the period of forty years of fruitless desert wandering but also strikes home with immediacy to the Hebrew Christians.

Through this passage, the Holy Spirit arcs across the centuries and speaks directly to the apostle's audience—and to us. It comes with urgency. *Today*—this is the key word that rings in the ear and to which the writer returns in 3:13 and again in 3:15 as he sounds warning.

What is "today"? It is God's eternal now. It is this moment, pregnant with divine warning and grace. It is this moment of opportunity. It is this moment to take stock and see where we are headed and to turn back to God's will for us.

Christianity is a religion of "todays." God calls His people ever onward, forward. He stirs us from our apathy and sluggishness; He challenges us to newness and growth. No Christian ever "has it made" in his or her spiritual journey. Moment by moment, day by day, we hear the call of the divine Spirit to press ahead, to "hold on to our courage and the hope of which we boast" (3:6).

In Hebrews 3, each of the three "today" appeals comes with a warning. Each one sets out the danger of hardening the heart. We will find one more "today" reference at 4:7, but there, Israel of old no longer will be in view, and the Spirit's appeal will come as an invitation rather than as a warning.

Ancient Israel rebelled against God, but before they defied God in act, they defied Him in spirit. The forty years of putting Yahweh to the test were the outworking of a spiritual condition. The author of Hebrews is more concerned about this condition in both the Israelites and his first century readers than he is with the behavior that derives from it. Notice how he describes the spiritual problem:

- "Do not harden your hearts" (vs. 8).
- "Their hearts are always going astray" (vs. 10).
- "A sinful, unbelieving heart that turns away from the living God" (vs. 12).
- "Hardened by sin's deceitfulness" (vs. 13).
- "Do not harden your hearts (vs. 15).
- "Because of their unbelief" (vs. 19).

Even while we are members of the people of God, a slow, insidious change may be taking place. Others may not know it, we may not know it, but God sees it. Our attitude to the Lord, our responsiveness to the Spirit, may be changing, not so much by open rejection as by neglect. Without wish or design, we may eventually find ourselves far from God's people—apostates and rebels.

Metallurgy gives us an illustration of the process. Steel may be softened by heating and worked into various configurations. Again and again it may be heated and reshaped in seemingly endless possibilities. But eventually the crystalline structure of the steel becomes permanently set, and it can no longer be reworked.

In the Christian life the divine Craftsman fashions us according to His blueprint. He sees great potential for us; He dreams a dream. Because of our stubbornness, we slow the process, but He does not give up shaping and fashioning us as we permit Him to proceed. Only our unwillingness delays the divine process, and only our unwillingness can negate it. If we continually refuse the divine Hand, eventually, like the steel that no worker, however skilled can reshape, we will harden ourselves into eternal rigidity.

The "hardening" process is slow—no one suddenly becomes a rebel. And it is subtle—sin's deceitfulness masks our eyes to what is happening within us. That's why every day the Holy Spirit must sound the urgent "Today!" That's why, when He sounds it in our ears, we must hear and heed.

Paul's warning in these verses elaborates the first application of Hebrews (2:1-3). Both passages describe a carelessness in religion, not an open rejection of Christ and His people. Chapter 3:12-15 with its description of the insidious change of heart expands our understanding of the consequences of ignoring "such a great salvation" in 2:3. The expression "the living God" (3:12) carries a note of judgment and retribution, paralleling "how shall we escape" in the first application (2:3). Elsewhere in Hebrews, we find the expression "the living God" associated with retribution (10:31; 12:22, 25).

We need to be clear, however, that the apostle's strong warning against falling away from God's plan for us does not leave us in a state of spiritual uncertainty. He speaks about courage and hope (3:6), encouraging one another (3:13), and confidence held firmly to the end (3:14).

So the Christian life set forth here isn't one of fearfulness and timidity, one that drags itself up the steep ascent to heaven, always unsure of its standing with God. No! It is an intelligent, alert experience that has gone beyond naiveté, that knows how deceitful is sin and how desperately wicked the human heart. But it goes forward confidently, boldly, because it rests on Christ's victory rather than our victory. Not in ourselves but in Him, not in our achievements but in His, not in what we are but in what He is—by fixing our thoughts on Him, we live in full assurance.

The final paragraph of the chapter, verses 16 to 19, focuses exclusively on the generation of Israelites that perished in the desert. They started well. They came out from Egypt in sight of God's uplifted hand, surrounded by evidences of divine leading and power. And they had a fine leader. Their failure cannot be placed at Moses' feet. He was, as 3:2-6a established, faithful in his discharge of the commission God gave him.

So two lessons emerge that are as important for God's people today as in the first century: Starting well and having a great leader cannot in themselves assure spiritual success. Everyone who confesses Christ starts well, regardless of the era, and every Christian has the finest Leader in the universe. But *we* each have a part to play. Like the Israelites of old, we may gradually turn our hearts from God and become rebels, and thus we may forfeit our place in the "Promised Land" that we have been seeking. In the Christian life, it is not better to travel hopefully than to arrive; attainment of eternal rest is our goal.

Some commentators have seen significance in the "forty years" quoted in Psalm 95:7-11 and mentioned again in Hebrews 3:17. They have speculated that, with Hebrews being written in the early sixties A.D., Christians again were thinking in terms of a forty-year period since Christ's death, with the second coming expected a few years hence. If Christians had such a time frame in view, the warning of 3:6-19 would come with particular thrust.

Although this idea has appeal, I do not find sufficient evidence in Hebrews to take it seriously. The apostle refers later to Christ's return (9:27, 28; 10:37, 38; 12:26, 27), but he does not refer to the forty years again. I think we had best understand the forty-year reference as a detail already present in the key passage, Psalm 95:7-11. Just as the writer plays on words like *today* and *harden* that he finds in the passage, so he picks up the forty years.

Some Seventh-day Adventist preachers have seen strong appli-

cation to the church in Hebrews 3:6b-19. Apart from the motivation to individual perseverance in the Christian way that we have
noticed, they have discerned broad parallels between the wandering Israelites and the Seventh-day Adventist movement. Speakers
and writers like Taylor G. Bunch have highlighted what they per-
ceived to be the failure of Adventists as a movement to fulfill God's
purposes. According to this line of thought, long ago, Adventists
should have completed the mission God gave them (to take the
everlasting gospel to the world), and Christ should have come.
Some statements from the pen of Ellen White support this view-
point, although others lead in a different direction, as they stress
the sovereignty and immutability of God's purposes. While this
application may have some validity, Hebrews does not suggest it.

The word for *rest* in the passage (vss. 11, 18) is the Greek
katapausis. So far as the wilderness generation is concerned, it
clearly referred to the land of Canaan, on which their hopes were
set. Two passages from the Pentateuch employ similar language
to that of Psalm 95:7-11 in expressing Yahweh's displeasure with
the rebellious Israelites. However, instead of *rest*, these texts refer
specifically to the Promised Land. One of them says: "When the
Lord heard what you said, he was angry and solemnly swore: 'Not
a man of this evil generation shall see the good land I swore to
give your forefathers' " (Deut. 1:34, 35; see also Num. 14:20-23).

If the apostle's discussion about *rest* closed with Hebrews 3, we
would have no question that his intent was earthly Canaan. In
chapter 4, however, we shall see how he continues to use this term
but takes it farther, giving it an application to his readers in the
first century (and by extension, to us).

The Old Testament story of Israel's failure highlights two ex-
ceptions: Joshua and Caleb remained faithful and alone survived
the forty years of wandering. Presumably the author of Hebrews
could have held them up as positive role models for the early
Christians. He does not, however. He draws out his arguments
from the wording of Psalm 95:7-11 rather than the Pentateuch.
Since the psalm focuses on the people en masse and fails to mention Joshua and Caleb, he likewise passes them by.

So the lesson from Israel's failure comes home forcefully to Christians. We also may fall short of the promised rest, which will be defined for us shortly (4:1-13). Despite all we have known and seen of God and His works, despite our superlative leader, despite belonging to the people of the new exodus, we may fail to attain our Promised Land. Only by heeding the urgent "today," only by obeying the voice of God in a faithful, persevering life, can we be assured of reaching the goal God has for us.

The final word of the chapter sums up the reason for Israel's failure: *unbelief* in the New International Version, but *apistia* in the Greek—literally, "*un*faith." The apostle repeats the point in 4:2: "Those who heard did not combine it [the gospel] with faith." Thus, whereas Hebrews 3 emphasizes the Israelites' *lack of faith*, Hebrews 4 will stress *faith* as the most important spiritual characteristic for Christian pilgrims.

Paul tells us much more about faith *(pistis)* in chapter 11, but we can rightly see the entire sermon as illustrating it. Although we wait until Hebrews 11 for our major study of the meaning of *faith*, the discussion of Hebrews 3 gives us several leading indications. *Faith* and its negative counterpart, *unfaith (unbelief)*, suggest two responses to God and His deeds. They point to two mind-sets, out of which two modes of conduct emerge.

Unfaith, apistia, has to be more than unbelief, since the term sums up the hardened heart, the person deceived by sin, who falls away from Yahweh and His goal. We see elements of inconstancy and lack of perseverance that take us far beyond mere absence of mental assent.

■ Getting Into the Word

Hebrews 4:1-13

Read Hebrews 4:1-13 twice. Then go back and read the entire section 3:1–4:13, noting how the ideas flow together. As you read, look for answers to these key questions that arise in 4:1-13:

1. What is the rest that "remains" for God's people today (4:9)? Since it cannot be earthly Canaan, what can it be?
2. Study the references to *rest* in 4:1-11. List them according to whether they indicate a *present* or a *future* rest.
3. How does the Sabbath feature in the discussion? Is the *rest* the Sabbath? Is the *rest* some other day? Does this passage provide evidence that the Hebrew Christians were observing the Sabbath?
4. Compare 4:8 in the New International Version with the King James Version. Which translation is correct? (The context will help you with the answer.)
5. What are the "works" from which we cease when we enter God's rest?
6. Study the "word of God" in 4:12, 13. Is the word of God a thing or a person?

■ Exploring the Word

Invitation to Faithfulness

The apostle develops his appeal through a closely reasoned passage (4:1-11) that requires careful and close thought to unpack. We can easily understand individual statements, but how each one relates to the next—that is the question. Yet, if we stay with this passage long enough, meditating prayerfully upon it, it will yield its logic, and we shall be richly rewarded.

Rest is the key word throughout these verses. We find the noun eight times (vss. 1, 3, 5, 6, 8, 10, 11). In every case, *rest* comes from the Greek word *katapausis*, the same word we noticed in 3:6b-19. At 4:9 we find a new word—one of high interest to Sabbath keepers—*sabbatismos*. It is translated "Sabbath-rest" in the New International Version. And we also find *rest* twice in the verb form (vss. 4, 10). In both these cases, *rested* corresponds to *katapausis*.

One can find a variety of interpretations of 4:1-11. Some

Seventh-day Adventists have seen here a specific injunction on behalf of the seventh-day Sabbath, while some Sunday keepers have found arguments on behalf of first-day observance!

A point we made early in our study of Hebrews applies with particular force here: Let the author reveal his meaning to us. Follow his reasoning through step by step, and then the meaning of specific statements will become clear. If we concentrate on this point or that without due consideration of context, we will distort his ideas. His thought, inspired by the Holy Spirit, proceeds in careful, logical stages and makes itself manifest to the unhurried student of the Word.

Before we try to answer the intriguing questions about *rest*, therefore, let us trace the steps in the argument of Hebrews 4:1-11. I see seven stages:

1. Only two groups of people are in view—those of Moses and of Jesus. From the wandering people of God in the desert, the apostle passes over in silence the intervening generations and leapfrogs to the Christians of the first century, to whom he writes. For him, Scripture speaks directly to the reader, transparent to the centuries that have passed.
2. He argues that the promise of rest still remains (vs. 1). Psalm 95:7-11 provides the basis for this argument. Its warning against hardening the heart and rebelling shows that God's promise is still unrealized.
3. But, the promise to enter rest must, at length, find fulfillment. "It still remains that some will enter that rest" (vs. 6), he tells us, stressing the absolute inevitability of the Word of God. That which Scripture states will happen must happen—if not at the time first promised, then in some future manifestation. God's Word accomplishes its purposes; it never returns to Him empty.
4. Any failure to enter rest comes from humanity, not from God. Israel in the desert fell short of the rest, but the rest was already there, provided by God. By implication, if any Christian fails to enter rest, the problem lies with him or her, not with

God. In fact, rest has always been available, right from Creation, as God's own resting demonstrates (vss. 3-5).

5. The wilderness generation failed because, although the rest was available and they had received the good news from God, they fell into unfaith and disobedience. And in similar fashion, Christians must be alert and take heed from Israel's experience.

6. Christians also must strive to enter God's rest, which still remains. They—the first-century people of God—and we are to respond to the divine call of the "today," avoiding the hardening of the heart and instead by faith entering into rest (vss. 3, 6, 9-11).

7. The concept of rest undergoes a transposition of meaning. In 3:6b-19 rest signifies no more than rest from enemies and trials in the land of Canaan. However, chapter 4:1-11 points out, on the basis of Psalm 95:7-11, that this rest has yet to be attained. So the apostle holds out a spiritual experience of rest for Christians, something already promised in Psalm 95:7-11, and toward which the readers must persevere.

Back of all these logical steps we see the Word of God. Because God has said it, it *will* come to pass; because God has promised, some of His people *will* realize the goal. And that Word speaks directly, immediately, to the ear. Spanning the centuries it is as real and vital now with its "*Today*, if you hear his voice" as when it first called men and women to God's goal.

I invite each reader to read and reread Hebrews 4:1-11 in light of the seven steps suggested above. Don't take my word for it. Test my analysis by the text. When the passage begins to feel comfortable—when it begins to seem like an old friend—then go on with me as we try to get to the bottom of this key word *rest*.

But What Is the "Rest"?

First, what about the *time* element here? Is the *rest* in this passage (4:1-11) present or future? Several statements suggest something that may be attained now:

- "We who have believed *enter* that rest" (4:3).
- "Anyone who *enters* God's rest also rests from his own work" (4:10).
- "It still remains that some will enter that rest. . . . Therefore God again set a certain day, calling it *Today*" (4:6-8).

Other points in the argument, however, point to the rest as still future:

- The invitation of 4:1-11 grows out of the lesson from Israel's failure in 3:6b-19, a passage that tilts toward the future. For the wandering tribes, the promise of rest (Canaan) was never fulfilled.
- The promise of entering rest "still stands" or "remains" (4:1, 6) suggesting that something has not yet been realized.
- The rest likewise "remains" (4:9).
- Christians are to be careful lest they, like Israel of old, "[fall] short" of entering God's rest (4:1).
- They are to "make every effort" to enter rest (4:11).

Thus, the *rest* of which Hebrews speaks seems to have both present and future elements almost evenly balanced. Can we make sense out of such an idea?

Yes, indeed! Throughout the New Testament, in fact, we find a balancing of what already has come through the life and death of Jesus Christ with what is yet to be. As early as the Gospels we encounter the concept in Jesus' teaching of the kingdom of God. In the words and deeds of Jesus, God's rule has broken through— the kingdom has come. "Blessed are the poor in spirit, for theirs *is* the kingdom of heaven" (Matt. 5:3). "If I drive out demons by the spirit of God, then the kingdom of God *has come* upon you" (Matt. 12:28).

At the same time, however, the kingdom in its fullness remains future. God's followers are to pray for the kingdom—"Your kingdom come" (Matt. 6:10); "come, you who are blessed by my Father; take your inheritance, the kingdom prepared for you since the creation of the world" (Matt. 25:34).

We often distinguish these two aspects of the kingdom by referring to the former as the "kingdom of grace" and the latter as the "kingdom of glory." These terms, while accurate in themselves, do not come from the Bible, which speaks simply of "the kingdom."

All the New Testament writings maintain this tension of "already" but "not yet" that the kingdom language portrays. With the coming of Jesus, *something* has happened! Salvation has come, grace abounds, the Spirit has been poured out, men and women have been forgiven, and Jesus even now reigns in the hearts of His followers. But the fullness of the divine purpose remains to be realized. Only when Jesus returns will every knee bow and acknowledge Him as King of kings and Lord of lords. Only then will the creation be restored to its pristine harmony. Only then will God's people be delivered from temptation, suffering, and death. Only then will Satan, whose head Jesus bruised on the cross, come to his final end. On Calvary, Jesus won the decisive battle in the age-long struggle between good and evil, but the war goes on. Soon, however, it will be over.

The book of Hebrews likewise steers a course between the "already" and the "not yet." We saw both elements in the opening paragraph (1:1-4). God's climactic speech has been given in the Son, who has made decisive purification of sins. At the same time, however, the Son awaits the full assumption of His lordship over the universe at the right hand of the Majesty of heaven.

Throughout Hebrews, this eschatological tension—"already" but "not yet"—will shape the discussion. As Paul argues about Jesus, our great High Priest and sacrifice, he will emphasize what He already has done and has made available for Christians even now. At the same time, however, he will show that God's people are still pilgrims and strangers on this earth on the way to the heavenly goal, living by hope. That is, the gospel comes to us as both fact and promise. So it is with rest in 4:1-11. God's people even now may enter it, but they will experience rest in its fullness only at the second coming.

We can now see more clearly what this rest entails. It is the bliss of salvation in Jesus Christ, into which we enter by faith in Him—a joy that is already a reality of Christians but that will attain an even deeper dimension in our eternal home with God.

The Rest and the Sabbath

The author's references to the Sabbath shed light on his meaning of *rest*. In 4:4 he picks up the idea of God's resting on the first Sabbath (Gen. 2:2) and carries the idea forward in 4:9—"There remains, then, a Sabbath-rest for the people of God." Throughout 3:6b–4:11, he used the same word for *rest—katapausis—* whether he was denoting the Old Testament goal of the wandering desert tribes or the new people of God. But at 4:9 we meet a word found nowhere else in the New Testament or the literature of the first century—*sabbatismos*, "Sabbath rest," "Sabbath-like rest," "Sabbath-ish rest."

I think the apostle coined this word to clinch the argument that began at 3:6b and comes to a climax at 4:9, 10. He clearly intends *sabbatismos* to be equivalent to *katapausis*, since he returns to that word in 4:10, but he wants to link the rest of which he speaks to the Sabbath.

Readers with a Jewish background probably would be quick to discern the link between rest and Sabbath. The rabbis taught that the Sabbath was more than a ceasing from labor; it was a foretaste of the age of the Messiah. Just so, the rest that God promises Christians may be entered into now but looks forward to full realization in the presence of God when Jesus returns.

With this understanding of 4:1-11, we can probe more closely several matters of deep interest to Sabbath keepers.

First, the passage furnishes no warrant for Sunday observance. The "another day" of 4:8 has nothing to do with Sabbath or Sunday. Rather, it ties in with the discussion about "today" in 4:7. The author's point is that God's invitation to His people at the time of Joshua remained unrealized, as is clearly evident by its repetition in Psalm 95:7-11 in David's time.

Perhaps, though, 4:1-11 supplies a direct appeal for Sabbath observance by equating rest with the Sabbath. Not quite. The Sabbath is an illustration of that rest. It has the *quality* of that rest. It is a Sabbath-ish rest. We may even say that the Sabbath is a part of that rest. But the rest itself is much more. It is an experience Christians can enjoy seven days a week that will reach its fullness only at the end of all things—the second coming.

In my judgment, Hebrews 4:1-11 gives us the strongest evidence in favor of the seventh-day Sabbath in the entire New Testament. Yet it does so without a direct appeal or invitation to keep the Sabbath. A direct appeal might suggest that the Hebrew Christians were debating which day to observe. But Hebrews introduces the Sabbath indirectly, in a nondefensive but highly positive manner. Our rest in Christ, says the author, has the *quality* of the Sabbath. It is *like* the Sabbath.

If, at the key point of his argument, in 4:9, 10, the writer associates rest with the Sabbath, two conclusions seem inescapable. First, for him and his readers, the Sabbath had a positive connotation. If they had considered it a burden, the last remains of a religion of bondage, the author would have lost his audience at this critical moment. Second, both he and his audience were keeping the Sabbath. They had no thought about any other day. Certainly they weren't debating the merits of Sabbath versus Sunday! Only in such a context could he call rest in Christ a *sabbatismos*.

In view of the rest in Christ, we can grasp the meaning of the apostle's statement about resting from one's own works in 4:10. The point of the analogy is simply the idea of cessation— as God ceased His work on the Sabbath, so we cease our work as we enter His rest. That work is the opposite of the way of faith. It is, as the discussion that began at 3:6b has shown, the evil, unbelieving heart, hardened by sin, that brings forth rebellion, disobedience, and unfaithfulness. In contrast to this way that marked ancient Israel, God holds out for us the way of faith, one that trusts God and goes forward with patience and perseverance.

Thus, Hebrews 4:10 does not contrast a system of righteousness by faith with one of righteousness by works. Nor does the

Christian's work, from which he or she ceases, correspond to God's creative acts. Instead, the text summarizes the two paths for the pilgrim, who is journeying toward the Promised Land: faith or unfaith.

As we conclude our discussion of 4:1-11, we should note two matters. The first already will have occurred to students familiar with the King James Version. In 4:8 the New International Version translates "Joshua," whereas the King James Version has "Jesus." Here, the New International Version surely is correct. The apostle is referring to the leader of the wandering tribes in 3:6b-19.

The second matter, practical in nature, points up the value of the apostle's ideas to life in our times. With our haste and nervous activity, our anxiety and stress, the promise of rest in Christ—rest to be entered *now*, in the midst of cares—has much appeal. Jesus issues a similar invitation: "Come to me, all you who are weary and burdened, and I will give you rest" (Matt. 11:28). The promise speaks powerfully to us all.

In the final verses of our passage, 4:12, 13, the writer returns to a note of warning. He describes the all-seeing eye of God, which is able to pierce to our innermost secrets and intentions. His word for disclosing the deepest springs of action—"laid bare" in the New International Version—comes from wrestling. It portrays the person who is pinned to the floor, utterly immobile and powerless.

His point, of course, reaches back to the admonition of 3:6b-19. We may fool others; we may even fool ourselves; but we cannot fool God. He sees; He knows. He can read our hearts. He can detect the beginnings of the hardening process that leads us far from His purposes.

As we read 4:12, 13, we notice a shift in subject. We begin with the Word of God that confronts us, searching our motives, as in Psalm 95:7-11. But in verse 13 the encounter is with God Himself—"him to whom we must give account." *God* speaks to us personally. Therefore, we should indeed "be careful that none of you be found to have fallen short of it" (vs. 1)!

■ Applying the Word

Hebrews 3:1–4:13

1. What difference does it make to me that Jesus is faithful? What difference does it make to the church? to the world?

2. How often do I think about Jesus and His accomplishment on my behalf? What changes do I need to make by His grace in order that I may practice the advice of Hebrews 3:1 and fix my thoughts on Him? How will my life be different when I have made those changes?

3. What will I do with "today"? What can I do that is new for Christ this today? What can I learn that is new? Will the world be a little better for my having been in it today? Will I be a little closer to heaven at the close of this day? How can I know that the answer to these questions is Yes?

4. Think of the time when you decided to be a Christian—of the glow of your first love, your earnestness, your strong desire to serve Him. How does your heart seem today? Has doubt found a place? love of the world? bitterness? If so, how did these traits enter, and how can you get rid of them?

5. Did I encourage someone today (Heb. 3:13)? Who do I know whom I might yet encourage? How can I encourage them?

6. How can I know that I am honest with God? with myself?

7. How do I feel about honestly saying the following prayer? "O Lord, open my eyes that I may see my need. Strip off my masks, painful though it will be, that I may see myself as You see me. And show me not only the wayward, doubting heart that is there but also the deep love with which You care for me and the value that You place on me."

8. What can I do to be sure that I enter Christ's rest now?

9. How does the following paragraph by Ellen White apply or not apply to me now? "Heaven is to begin on this earth. When the Lord's people are filled with meekness and

tenderness, they will realize that His banner over them is love, and His fruit will be sweet to their taste. They will make a heaven below in which to prepare for heaven above" (White, *Testimonies*, 7:131).

10. To what extent is the Sabbath a divine command to me? a requirement for my salvation? a foretaste of heaven for me? a sample of the salvation Christ already has brought to me?

11. In what ways has God's Word, the Bible, spoken to me personally and directly? How has it encouraged and warned me? In what ways do I, like Jesus, live " 'on every word that comes from the mouth of God' " (Matt. 4:4)?

■ Researching the Word

1. With the help of a concordance, look up the word *rest* in the Old Testament. Trace the use of this word from its application to earthly Canaan in the time of Joshua through later uses. Then go back to Hebrews 3:7–4:11 and study how the concept of rest develops even further. Compare what you have learned with the words of Jesus in Matthew 11:28-30. What spiritual significance do you see to the word *rest* that you did not understand before?

2. Review the story of Israel's failure to enter the land of Canaan in Numbers 13 and 14. Next, review the spiritual lessons that Paul draws from this story in Hebrews 3:12-17. What additional lessons come to your mind from details of the story in Numbers that Paul does not mention in Hebrews? How can these lessons help you in your effort to be a believing Christian?

■ Further Study of the Word

1. For a thorough, detailed study of Hebrews 3:1–4:13, see B. F. Westcott, *The Epistle to the Hebrews*, 72-105. (Note: Westcott makes continual reference to the Greek text.)

2. For a clear commentary on the text but with fewer technical details, see F. F. Bruce, *The Epistle to the Hebrews*, rev. ed., 90-117.

3. For an exposition on the Sabbath, see Ellen G. White, *The Desire of Ages*, 281-289.

The Better Priest

Hebrews 4:14–6:20

In this section the apostle develops and expands the theme of Jesus as High Priest that he first mentioned in 2:17—"In order that he might become a merciful and faithful high priest in service to God." His faithfulness as high priest was again elaborated in 3:1-6. In 4:14–6:20 the emphasis falls on the merciful aspects of Christ's priestly ministry.

The argument in this section falls into two distinct parts: 4:14–5:10, where Paul discusses the high-priestly motif, and 5:11–6:20, where he breaks off that line of thought to bring an extended application of warning and encouragement.

■ Getting Into the Word

Hebrews 4:14–5:10

Read Hebrews 4:14–5:10 three times. Ignore the break between chapters—it was added many centuries later. The theme of Jesus as our great High Priest runs throughout these verses, and they should be studied as a unit. After you have prayerfully and thoughtfully considered the passage, go back and consider it once more in light of the following questions:

1. Does the idea of Jesus as High Priest seem strange to you? What positive aspects do you find in 4:14-16?
2. What does "tempted in every way" (4:15) mean? Did Jesus

go through all the temptations we face? Did He have a nature that could be enticed by sin?

3. What needs do we have that the apostle mentions in 4:16? How does Jesus' high-priestly ministry in the heavenly sanctuary meet those needs? Is the emphasis more on forgiveness of sin or on help with overcoming sin? Explain your answer?

4. Study the description of the Aaronic high priests in 5:1-4 and list the characteristics that the apostle sets out for us.

5. With the aid of a concordance, look up the following high priests in the Bible: Eli, Pashur, Annas, and Caiaphas. Read their stories, and find out all you can about them from a Bible dictionary. In what ways did they live up to the description of a high priest in Hebrews 4:1-4? In what ways did they fail to live up to this description?

6. Now compare the account of Jesus as our High Priest in 5:5-10 with the description of the Aaronic high priests in 5:1-4. Which points from 5:1-4 does the apostle highlight concerning Jesus? Why?

7. What experiences in the life of Jesus come to your mind in the account of 5:7-9?

8. Study carefully the logic of 5:5, 6, where God designates Jesus as High Priest. How do the two quotations from the Old Testament come together to establish Jesus' high priesthood?

9. We will find Psalm 110 referred to many times in Hebrews, with verse 4 emerging as *the* key text from the Old Testament for this book. Look up this psalm, and note carefully the role of verse 4 in it.

10. Notice how Hebrews 4:14–5:10 elaborates further on three great ideas about Jesus that we saw already in our discussion of 2:5-18—suffering, testing (tempting), and perfecting. What have you learned in your study thus far that might clarify the strange expression "he learned obedience" in 5:8 so it makes more sense to you now?

■ Exploring the Word

Hebrews 4:14–5:10 has two distinct parts. In 4:14-16 the apostle gives an overall statement about Jesus as our great High Priest and what that means to us. In 5:1-10 he compares and contrasts Jesus and Aaron.

Our Great High Priest

Hebrews 4:14-16 has inspired preachers and encouraged students of Hebrews for centuries. Succinct, direct, packed with pregnant phrases, it stands out as one of the most precious passages in the entire New Testament. We must take our time here, reflecting, pondering, marveling at what God has for us as He discloses the marvel of our great High Priest.

Our faith rests on something solid, on *Someone*—that is the apostle's first point. We *have* a great high priest in heaven, and He guarantees that what we profess isn't a matter of feeling or philosophy, of speculation or possibility. At the heart of our religion stands a Man, and His name is Jesus—a Man, but much more, for He is God's Son!

That is why we should hold firm in our confession. That is why we haven't followed "cleverly invented stories" (2 Pet. 1:16). That is why we can stand unshaken and unmoved amid the storms of doubt, skepticism, and relativity that wash over planet Earth in our day.

But this Jesus whom we confess, although truly God, isn't some remote deity. He draws near to us, sympathizing with us in our hurts and our brokenness—this is the apostle's second great idea. This Jesus comes to us, not as an avenging deity, but as a merciful high priest! Just as Jesus, during the time of His earthly ministry, had compassion on the harried, worried men and women of Galilee (Matt. 9:36), so now, in heaven above, He opens His arms to receive us in our pain and loneliness. He understands; He cares; He identifies with us.

For our great High Priest knows how it feels to be human. He knows what it means to suffer, to struggle with the powers of evil. He knows even the experience of death itself. He knows, not because as the Son of God He can access all knowledge, but because He has lived—and died—as a human being. Just as He *is* real (we *have* a great high priest), so His human experiences *were* real. God didn't give Him easy answers or an easy way out. God didn't write the script of His life so that He couldn't succumb to the test. No, He went through it all just as we go through it all, and the help He now offers us as High Priest is as genuine as the suffering He endured.

We struggle to grasp these ringing affirmations. We want to ask, How could He be tempted, since He was God in the flesh? How could He be tempted *in every way* like us, since He lived so long ago, in a different age and place?

The apostle does not spell out answers to our questions. He merely affirms that the One who forms the foundation of our confession, the One who is our heavenly High Priest, sympathizes with us in our brokenness and struggles because He has been through experiences similar to ours. But elsewhere he gives us additional information that keeps us from wrong conclusions and helps us piece together the puzzle of Jesus, the God-Man.

He tells us, for instance, that our High Priest is "holy, blameless, pure, set apart from sinners" (7:26). He tells us that, unlike the Aaronic high priests, Jesus had no need to offer sacrifices for His own sins (vs. 27). So we may be sure that our Lord did not have a corrupted nature that hankered after sin, that preferred the darkness to the light, and to which the devil could appeal with his enticements.

Perhaps we need to paint the temptations of Jesus on a broader canvas. We often portray them as examples for our struggles for individual piety. In this endeavor, noble as it is, we can easily reduce Christian living to something essentially negative—an elimination or overcoming of a list of sins. But the life to which the Master calls us—the One that He modeled for us—wasn't an *absence* of sins but one of wholeness. It was a positive outflow of deeds and words springing from a heart in tune with the heavenly

Father. In that living, He confronted temptation, and the tests were real and the struggles severe. But the issue was His relationship to the Father's will. Would He abide in the divine plan, or would He take the shortcut the devil offered Him? Would He drink the cup of rejection, sorrow, and pain, or would He seek an easy way out?

So Jesus was tested "in every way, just as we are." The basic issue in temptation is the same today as it was two thousand years ago: Will we keep trusting God, seeking to follow His plan? Will we honor Him, putting Him and what He stands for first? It matters not that Jesus wasn't exposed to some areas of temptation that we face, or that He encountered some we will never meet. Jesus was truly human and shared our human experiences, so He was one with us in suffering and test.

Unlike us, however, Jesus remained sinless through every confrontation with evil. He was without sin, and He did no sin. Our great High Priest is without flaw, and so, as we will see later in the argument of Hebrews, the sacrifice He offers—Himself—is a perfect sacrifice.

Because we have such a high priest, the doors of heaven's temple swing open wide to welcome us. The command center of the universe no longer holds fear and uncertainty for us—we *belong* there. We come confidently (King James Version: "boldly") into the divine presence. This is Paul's final point in this marvelous passage. The word translated "approach" in verse 16 is the Greek *proserchomai*, which was used for the high priest's entry into the Most Holy Place (see also Heb. 10:22 for the same word).

With this development, we meet, for the first time, a key idea of Hebrews—access. In the theological summit of the book, 9:1–10:18, we will see this thought explained and expanded.

Hebrews 4:14-16 echoes 2:18—"Because he himself suffered when he was tempted, he is able to help those who are being tempted." Both set forth a winning portrait of Jesus as High Priest, One who understands and cares because of His experiences shared with us. And both close with the thought that He is able to help us in our time of need—when we are being tested.

The help our High Priest offers, then, is primarily overcoming help. No doubt Paul would not exclude forgiveness (the mention of *mercy* in 4:16, as in 2:17, allows for it), but this isn't his logical conclusion. Rather, He who overcame in the fires of human tests stands ready to aid us in the same sort of tests that we, too, may emerge successful.

Christ and Aaron

In 5:1-4 the apostle begins with a brief description of the Aaronic high priests. The author's account lists the following characteristics:

1. The high priest is appointed by God to the office—one cannot take the honor upon himself (vss. 1, 4).
2. He comes from "among men," that is, he represents humanity in this office (vs. 1).
3. He plays a mediatorial role, since he acts on behalf of humanity (vs. 1).
4. He offers "gifts and sacrifices"—that is, he serves in a sacrificial context for the people (vs. 1). Scholars customarily employ the term cult or cultus for this sacrificial context. The word when used this way has nothing to do with deviant Christian groups.
5. He also fulfills a function for the removal of sins (atonement), since the sacrifices are "for sins" (vs. 1).
6. He "deal[s] gently" with human frailty, because he is aware of his own weakness (vs. 2).
7. He needs to offer sacrifice for his own sins as well as for those of the people (vs. 3).

Thus, we discern seven aspects of the high priest's role: divine appointment, representation, mediation, cultic function, atonement, compassion for others, and sacrifice for his own sins.

As we think back over the story of Israel as the Old Testament presents it, we realize that the account in Hebrews 5:1-4 gives us an idealized portrait of the high priest. Many high priests seemed to forget that God had appointed them—they simply took their office for granted, because their birth placed them in Aaron's line. Nor do we find them "dealing gently" with the ignorant and wayward and keenly conscious of their own need of sacrifice. Instead, we read of Eli's sons, who flaunted their immoral conduct and were greedy for the spoils of office (1 Sam. 2:12-17); or of Pashur, who opposed the prophet Jeremiah and put him in the stocks (Jer. 20:1-6).

By the time of Jesus, the high-priestly office had sunk to an all-time low. From the time of the Hasmoneans (142 to 37 B.C.), the office of high priest had become a powerful political, as well as a religious, post. Individuals plotted, bribed, and murdered to obtain it. In Jesus' day it was in the hands of the Sadducees, who, incredible as it seems, were a secularized sect of the Jews who accepted only the first five books of the Bible (the Pentateuch) and did not believe in the resurrection or angels (see Matt. 22:23; Acts 23:8).

In Hebrews 5:1-4, Paul does not contrast this sorry state of affairs with Jesus' high-priestly ministry. Rather, he presents the high priests at their best for comparison and contrast with Jesus. His purpose is to show that even in its ideal state, the Aaronic office falls far short of our great High Priest.

The next six verses, 5:5-10, turn the spotlight on Jesus. Here we find, not a point-by-point comparison based on the list above, but concentration on just two features of the seven: divine appointment and mercy.

First, Paul argues that, like Aaron, Jesus became High Priest by divine appointment. As God once called Aaron to be high priest for Israel, thus making him first of a long line in the priestly office, so He called Christ. "You are a priest forever," Paul wrote (quoting from the Psalms). Long before Jesus came on the scene, while the Aaronic priesthood still flourished, Scripture predicted that a new priest would one day appear, One whom God would appoint to an entirely new order.

In Hebrews 7 the apostle will focus on this new order, of which

Christ is High Priest. Using Psalm 110:4 as the key, with rigorous analysis, he will demonstrate the weakness of the old order and the superiority of the new.

However, already in 5:5-10 he includes something we shouldn't overlook. To say that Jesus became a High Priest by divine appointment just like Aaron is only half correct. True, in both cases, God designates, but the case of Jesus brings in a major new element.

Notice the logic of 5:5, 6. We would expect the reasoning to proceed like this: "So Christ also did not take upon himself the glory of becoming a high priest. But God said to him, 'You are a priest forever, in the order of Melchizedek.' " This would be straightforward and clear.

But that isn't what we find. In making the appointment to high-priestly office, God *first* says to Christ: "You are my Son; today I have become your Father." This is the primary divine declaration that designates Jesus as High Priest. The second statement, from Psalm 110:4, although important, is clearly secondary, as shown by the manner of its introduction: "And [or also] he says in another place."

We begin to understand the reasoning in light of 7:28—"The oath [that is, of Psalm 110:4], which came after the law, appointed the Son, who has been made perfect forever." *Because Christ is the Son, He may be designated as High Priest.* We saw in 2:5-18 how Paul stressed the necessity of human experiences for Jesus to become High Priest; but we must remember that He was God's Son before He became the son of Mary. That is, the Son alone is the person to be designated as High Priest after He becomes human and is perfected by suffering.

So the divine appointment of Jesus brings as much contrast with Aaron as it does comparison. Both are constituted high priests by God's declaration, and both are human. In these two ways, they are similar. But the priesthood to which Jesus is called demands much more—something for which Aaron and his descendants could never qualify: divine *Sonship*.

This thought deserves profound reflection. Hebrews presents

a conception of priesthood that radically alters our previous understanding. Now we see that, while Aaron and all his fellow high priests of the Old Testament shared some features in common with Christ, a vast gulf separates them from Him. He alone is the true High Priest, for in Him alone, deity and humanity combine; the Aaronic high priests are but faint representations or illustrations of the great High Priest—*the one and only true Priest*—who would at length appear.

Because Christ is Son, He has access to the very presence of God, to the eternal world, where angels are but servants to the throne of grace. Because He became human, He links irrevocably to us, sympathetic, merciful, helping us in our struggles.

Now we can see more clearly how the profound theology of this book comes together. The first chapter argues emphatically for the true, eternal deity of the Lord. The second, in sharp contrast, presents Him in the Incarnation as a little lower than angels, suffering, tested, dying—the Son became our "brother." These two streams—the divine and the human—meet in the God-Man, our great High Priest.

Think of the implications. Only *one* true Priest, now and forever. Every other priest but a shadow, an illustration of Him.

How careful we should be of using the term *priest* of any other! How misguided is any individual or any human system that would seek to take the place of our great High Priest!

Jesus. Alone. Unique. All our hopes in this life and the next center in Him!

In contrast to the focus on Sonship in 5:5, 6, the next four verses take up once more Jesus' humanity. They run parallel to the account of 2:5-18 and may be seen as an elaboration of 4:15—"For we do not have a high priest who is unable to sympathize with our weaknesses, but we have one who has been tempted in every way, just as we are—yet was without sin."

Paul uses vivid words here: *prayers, petitions, loud cries, tears*. His description reminds us of Jesus' Gethsemane agony and indeed is the most graphic picture of Jesus' sufferings apart from the Gospels' account of Jesus in the garden.

There is no make-believe here, no playacting, no stolid, stoic calm in the jaws of death. With pleas and loud entreaties, Jesus prayed to be delivered, and God heard Him.

One famous scholar, Adolf von Harnack, puzzled over 5:7 and concluded that a word must be missing from the text. Since Jesus prayed to be saved from death and yet did go to death, He could not have been heard. So von Harnack inserted—entirely without support of any ancient manuscript—the word *not*: "And he was not heard."

But von Harnack missed the point. In Gethsemane, Jesus three times prayed, "My Father, if it is possible, may this cup be taken from me. Yet not as I will, but as you will" (Matt. 26:39). God *did* hear Jesus' prayer, but His answer was No. Only by going to the cross and to death could the Son win our salvation.

The New International Version also misses the point on Hebrews 5:8. In light of verse 5, the translation shouldn't be "although he was *a* son, but "although he was *the* Son." The New English Bible captures accurately the apostle's thinking: "son though he was." The *although* makes clear that we are dealing with a seeming contradiction. Here is One who is the Son—that is, equal with God—and yet He learns obedience. If we translate as in the New International Version, the *although* loses any meaning, for we expect every "son" (every human being) to learn obedience.

But even though He was God's Son, Jesus learned new levels of submission to the divine will—He "learned obedience." Through temptation and suffering, He became qualified to be the source of eternal salvation—He was "made perfect."

Son He was eternally, but through the Incarnation, He shared our human lot. Thus God could designate Him, the God-Man, as our great High Priest.

We can now review the seven characteristics of Aaronic high priests in 5:1-4 in light of the account of Jesus in 5:5-10. While we find some similarities, the overwhelming thrust is contrast. We have a *better* high priest.

Aaron	Christ
1. Appointed by God.	1. Appointed by God— but *because* He is the Son!
2. Comes from "among men."	2. The Son *became* man.
3. Mediatorial role.	3. Not mentioned here.
4. Sacrificial (cultic) function.	4. Not mentioned here.
5. Functions for sin's removal (atonement).	5. Not mentioned here.
6. Deals gently with human frailties.	6. Merciful, sympathetic.
7. Needs to sacrifice for own sins.	7. Not mentioned here, but specifically denied in 7:26-28.

Of the seven points, then, one is specifically denied (sinfulness), three are significantly modified (divine appointment of the Son, not merely a man but God incarnated, and sympathetic because He passed through extreme human experiences), and three are left undeveloped. These last three, however—Christ as humanity's representative and His sacrificial (cultic) and atoning ministry—will form the backdrop for the later discussion of our great High Priest in the heavenly sanctuary (8:1–10:18).

■ Getting Into the Word

Hebrews 5:11–6:20

Read Hebrews 5:11–6:20 twice, carefully and prayerfully. As you read, seek for the answers to each of the following questions:

1. **What does this passage indicate about the original readers of Hebrews?**
2. **How does Paul deal with the spiritual sluggishness of the Hebrews?**
3. **Have the Christians described in 6:4-6 received such unusual blessings that they are without hope if they fall away from Christ?**

4. Hebrews 6:4-6 has troubled Christians from the early centuries. In seeking to understand it, look at two other passages in Hebrews that seem to parallel it: 10:26-31 and 12:15-17. Does Hebrews teach that those who apostatize can never return to Christ? Explain your answer.
5. What are the "two unchangeable things" that encourage God's people (vs. 18)?
6. Hebrews 6:19 has been at the center of controversy concerning the doctrine of the sanctuary held by Seventh-day Adventists. The crucial issue concerns the meaning of "within the veil" (Kings James Version). Note that the New International Version's translation—"the inner sanctuary behind the curtain"—introduces ideas not found in the original Greek, which is literally "the inner of the veil." In dealing with this key text, try to figure out:
   a. Why the passage has involved so much discussion and controversy.
   b. What is "the veil" (curtain)?
   c. What point is the apostle trying to make?

■ Exploring the Word

The discussion of Jesus as heavenly High Priest, one like Aaron in some respects but infinitely greater, breaks off suddenly. From 5:11 through chapter 6, the author chides his hearers for their slowness to learn and warns them against falling away. Only at the end of the chapter does he bring the subject back to Jesus' priestly ministry.

This long application—the third one in the book—comes in two parts. In 5:11–6:8 Paul issues a rebuke and strong warning, but then in 6:9-20 he turns to an encouraging note.

A Passage That Perplexes and Troubles Many

Paul has material "hard to explain" for his readers—presumably the Melchizedekian priesthood, because this is where he suddenly shuts down the theological discussion (5:10) and where he eventually picks it up again (6:20). But they aren't ready. They have failed to grow in understanding and are still babes when they ought to be teachers.

The Hebrews, then, have been Christians for some time. They cannot be new converts, and far less can they be Jews who haven't yet accepted Christ, as some commentators have suggested.

Thus, we see a development beyond the previous applications. Whereas 2:1-4 and 3:7–4:13 highlight the dangers of the Hebrews drifting away from the faith or their hearts becoming hardened by the deceitfulness of sin, here we find the apostle's concern, not only over what *might* happen to them, but over what already *has* happened.

"Slow to learn"—this is how he describes them (5:11). The Greek word is *nōthros*, which means "blunt," "dull," "sluggish," "remiss," or "slack." We could describe their problem as "tired blood"; and the diagnosis sounds surprisingly contemporary! Far too many contemporary Christians, who have followed the Lord for years, find that the fizz has gone out of their spiritual life. Inert and indifferent, they need a transfusion of divine enthusiasm.

How Paul deals with this spiritual condition is fascinating and instructive. Although he broke off the theological discussion about Jesus as High Priest because the Hebrews were unprepared for it and needed milk instead of solid food, he nevertheless says, "Therefore let us leave the elementary teachings about Christ and go on to maturity" (6:1). How can this be? Even though they are ready only for "milk," will he give them the "solid food" anyway? Won't this cause spiritual indigestion?

I think his meaning is this: while the Hebrews haven't developed spiritually as much as he would have liked, and thus apparently lack the maturity for what he has to offer, nevertheless, "solid food" alone will help them. And indeed he does give them heavy fare. The discussion of chapter 7 is one of the most involved in the entire New Testament! I don't think Paul divides his audience so that the mature among them will learn from what he is about to present (as some commentators suggest). Rather, he believes that their tired spiritual blood can only be rejuvenated by the consideration of Jesus that he has for them.

Sometimes Christians, and even some preachers, put down theology as impractical. We all do well to ponder Paul's approach here. Obviously, he believes in intellectual stimulation, in feeding the flock with theological ideas that will stretch their minds. Of course, these ideas aren't an end in themselves. His concern is to arouse their spiritual energies—a highly practical goal. But we ought to stake out the point: For some spiritual needs, *only* a theological treatment can help! Ellen White has statements along similar lines. Although occasionally some voices advocate a mindless type of Christianity, she advocates stretching our intellects, referring positively to "intellectual Christian[s]" (*Counsels to Parents, Teachers, and Students*, 361).

The apostle follows the rebuke of 5:11-14 with a severe warning. This passage, 6:4-6, reminds us of the third angel's message of Revelation 14:9-12 in its apparently uncompromising stance. From the earliest centuries of the Christian era, these verses have troubled and terrified God's people. Because 6:4-6 seems to deny repentance for sins committed after baptism, the practice arose of putting off baptism until one's deathbed! A second-century writing, *The Shepherd of Hermas*, in obvious reaction to the passage, modified the idea to permit one—but only one—lapse after baptism! The lawyer-writer Tertullian, also in that century, tried to limit the text by applying its strictures to sexual offenses!

Earnest Christians will struggle with 6:4-6. Scholars and commentators still have a difficult time seeking to understand it. Some try to make *impossible* mean "difficult" (which it doesn't) or translate the final clause as "*while* they are crucifying the Son of God all over again" (which makes the statement so obvious as to be meaningless).

I think we should begin by letting Scripture interpret itself. The apostle repeats the ideas of 6:2-6 in two other places: 10:26-31 and 12:15-17. While the form of each varies, each passage contains the same severe warnings against open, public rejection of Christ.

1. **Privileges:**
   6:4-6—Enlightened, tasted heavenly gift, partakers of Holy Spirit, tasted Word of God, coming age.
   10:26-31—Knowledge of the truth, blood of the new covenant, Spirit of grace.
   12:15-17—The birthright.
2. **Offense:**
   6:4-6—Commit apostasy.
   10:26-31—Sin deliberately.
   12:15-17—Despise the birthright.
3. **Result:**
   6:4-6—Impossible to restore to repentance.
   10:26-31—No more sacrifice for sins.
   12:15-17—No chance to repent.
4. **Prospect of divine judgment:**
   6:4-6—Curse, burning (see vss. 7, 8).
   10:26-31—"Fearful expectation of judgment" worse than for the violators of Moses' law; falling into the "hands of the living God."
   12:15-17—Rejection (see also vs. 29—"consuming fire").
5. **Reasons for divine rejection:**
   6:4-6—"Crucifying the Son of God all over again and subjecting him to public disgrace."
   10:26-31—"Trampled the Son of God under foot . . . treated as an unholy thing the blood of the covenant . . . insulted the Spirit of grace."
   12:15-17—"Godless."

We find the same elements in each of the three passages; the emphasis merely shifts. In 6:4-6 the focus falls on spiritual privileges, in 10:26-31 on judgment, and in 12:15-17 on the impossibility of rehabilitation.

As we consider the privileges listed in the three passages, we do not find indications that those whom the apostle warns have been given unique blessings by the Lord. They are not a select group among Christians, for whom any lapse would signal a reprehensible failure to appreciate the gifts that God has bestowed upon them. No, the privileges outlined are the birthright of everyone who accepts Jesus Christ as Saviour and Lord—the enlightenment of the Holy Spirit, the foretaste of heaven, the power of the indwelling Christ, the heirship to eternal glory.

Thus the sin against which the apostle warns is one that any Christian may commit. Recognition of this point, coupled with the seemingly hopeless condition described in the three passages, has caused Christians much puzzlement and anxiety. Let us take up 6:4-6 and see if the context helps advance our understanding of these heavy words.

First, we note that 6:4-6 comes in the middle of a sermonic application. While it contains theological elements, it is not part of a careful argument that seeks to spell out the nature of the "unpardonable sin." Second, Paul specifically excludes his readers from among those who fall away from Christ. He says he is "persuaded [of] better things [concerning] you" (6:9). Third, we note the *if* in verse 6 that puts the whole discussion on a conditional basis.

What Paul is presenting is a *possibility* rather than an actual situation. As we consider his strong words in light of the earlier applications (2:1-4; 3:1–4:13), we see that the scenario of 6:4-6 is the logical end result of the spiritual tendencies he sees among the Hebrews. Already they are in danger of drifting from the goal, of becoming hardened through sin's deceitfulness. Already they have failed to grow into the stature the Lord intends for them. So because of present neglect of divine opportunities, they could—as unthinkable as it might seem—one day come to the point of outright, public rejection of the Lord.

The picture Hebrews paints isn't one of lapses from the divine will that every Christian continually encounters—those falls and shortcomings that arise from the weaknesses of our nature and the buffetings of the evil one. Instead, the apostle presents a scene of deliberate renunciation: As once men and women accepted Jesus, now they publicly disown Him.

In the West we don't find this scene played out very often. Most

Christians who fall away simply stop coming to church and cease trying to live as followers of Christ. Rarely do they declare that they want nothing more to do with Him.

For the early Christians, however, that possibility was real and not infrequently witnessed. Until the fourth century, Christians had no legal standing in the Roman Empire. They weren't permitted to build places of worship (hence the house churches) and could be arrested, tried, and executed simply because of their profession of Jesus. Sporadic waves of persecution washed over them during these centuries, and with each test, some Christians publicly renounced Christ by offering incense to Caesar as god or by declaring, "Caesar is Lord."

I saw a roughly parallel situation in India. Among India's eight hundred million people, Christians are a small minority—only about 2 percent. The culture focuses on the festivals of the dominant religion, Hinduism, and to some extent on those of Islam. So Christmas and Easter come and go without carols or trees, without colored lights, the *Messiah*, Scrooge, or the *Nutcracker Suite*. Further, a militant sect of Hinduism works to counter the spread of Christianity and to attract Christians back into the Hindu fold. Newspaper reports tell of public gatherings organized by Hindus where erstwhile followers of Jesus turn their backs on Him.

This sort of scenario, I expect, lies behind the severe warning of Hebrews. It runs in a different channel from the teachings of Jesus that point out the sin God cannot forgive. His words (Mark 3:23-27) came in the context of religious leaders who attributed His miracles and exorcisms to the power of Satan. By doing so, they rejected the Holy Spirit who had anointed the Master's ministry and thereby cut themselves off from the Source of conviction, repentance, and salvation.

Students of Hebrews at times marvel at the radical contrasts of this book. Here, we find the strongest words of Christian assurance coupled with the strongest warnings to Christians. But the two go together. When we see how wonderful Jesus is and how precious is His saving death and ministry for us, then—and only then—do we realize how heinous an act it is to treat lightly His grace or to spurn it.

The illustration from nature in 6:7, 8 drives home this point. Land that receives God's blessings should bring forth corresponding fruit; if it doesn't, it is useless. So don't deal carelessly with divine privileges.

An Encouraging Word

With Hebrews 6:9 the apostle's mood changes suddenly. He praises the Hebrews for their good works (vss. 9-12) and closes the application with the certainty of God's promises (vss. 13-20).

Hebrews 6:11, 12 encapsulates the purpose of the sermon: "We want each of you to show this same diligence to the very end, in order to make your hope sure. We do not want you to become lazy, but to imitate those who through faith and patience inherit what has been promised." *Diligence, patience, hope, faith, promise—* these words sum up the practical concerns that lie behind the book.

The final paragraph sets out the absolute certainty of God's promise. Here, Abraham appears as an example that illustrates both the nature of the divine promise and the appropriate human response to it. When God promised Abraham's descendants the land (Gen. 22:16, 18), He made His word doubly sure: He promised, and He confirmed the promise by an oath. And Abraham did his part: He "patiently endured" (Heb, 6:15, KJV) and so received the promise.

We Christians are also children of promise. In this life the gospel comes to us as hope. Only later will we realize its full dimensions (see 11:1-40). But God gives to us a twofold assurance, as He gave it to Abraham—He promises, and He adds His oath. In this case the oath must be that of Psalm 110:4—"The Lord has sworn and will not change his mind: 'You are a priest forever, in the order of Melchizedek.' "

Once again the author has introduced an idea on which he will shortly expound. In 7:19-22 he will refer specifically to this oath, and once again he will couple it with hope.

Chapter 6 closes with a ringing affirmation. When Christians hope, it isn't a blind optimism, a buoyancy of spirit, a mere whistling in the dark. Our hope rests on *facts*, on *realities*. Jesus anchors our hopes. His person and His work make our salvation absolutely sure.

In these cynical and pessimistic years that march toward the close of the old millennium, "*We have this hope*"! Steady, sure, steadfast, firm—because Jesus is our Anchor. Oh, how great is His salvation, how precious the life He now gives us, with the promise held out before us that the best is yet to come!

Our hope, says Paul, reaches to the very presence of God. It is grounded in the heavenly sanctuary itself, where Jesus ministers as our great High Priest. We grasp these words, and they buoy us up amid life's tempests.

Within the Veil

Paul's expression, translated as "the inner sanctuary behind the curtain" (6:19) in the NIV, raises new and peculiarly Adventist questions. We need to look at his words carefully, seeking to understand why Adventists and their opposers have directed so much energy toward this passage. In order to avoid prejudicing the result, we will revert to the more literal and therefore neutral translation of the King James Version, "within the veil."

About eighty years ago, a privately published book appeared with the arresting title *Cast Out for the Cross of Christ*. Its author, Albion Foss Ballenger, had been a Seventh-day Adventist minister of some influence. Now he was outside the ministry and outside the Adventist fold. Ballenger argued extensively from Hebrews, asserting that this book sees the cross as the antitypical day of atonement. The key to Ballenger's thesis was the phrase *within the veil*.

In fact, the history of Seventh-day Adventist thought is strewn with controversy over the issue that Ballenger brought to prominence. As early as 1846, O. R. L. Crosier felt the force of the problem, and in 1877, Uriah Smith gave consideration to it. In *Seventh-day Adventism Renounced*, D. M. Canright argued that Jesus entered the Most Holy Place at His ascension, not in 1844. W. W. Fletcher, an Australian church leader who also left the church, listed this matter as one of the main reasons for his defection. In recent year, Desmond Ford argued for a similar interpretation.

Thus, Hebrews has often emerged as a storm center among Adventist interpreters. Here, beyond any other writing of the New Testament, we find a detailed discussion of Jesus' sacrificial death. The stakes are high for us Seventh-day Adventists because of our belief in the heavenly sanctuary, with Jesus entering upon the final (second apartment) phase of His ministry in 1844. But if Hebrews sets forth Calvary as the New Testament Day of Atonement, what becomes of 1844? Then Hebrews, to which we have appealed for support of our most distinctive doctrine, becomes our theological Waterloo.

We will fully address the key passages—which alone can provide the answer—when we take up Hebrews 8:1–10:18, the theological summit of the book and also the heart of the sacrificial argumentation. We shall endeavor to be honest with the Word, facing difficulties squarely and not seeking an easy way out. For we believe, indeed are *certain*, that the Lord will lead us into His light if we earnestly seek to find it.

Leaving discussion of the larger issue for later (chapter 7—"The Better Blood"), let us look briefly at Ballenger's reasoning concerning "within the veil." Readers who wish to pursue the matter in more detail may consult the additional source materials listed at the end of this chapter.

Ballenger considered the various words for *veil* in both the Hebrew and the Greek, and also the expression associated with the veil. He summarized his conclusions:

> Now, if the Scripture in Heb. 6:19 had said that Christ had entered the "first veil," then the question would be settled; but he simply says that Christ has entered "within the veil." Now, inasmuch as he uses the term without explaining it, taking it for granted that his readers

understand to what place he refers, the all-important question arises: To which place—within the first veil, or within the second veil—would the reader understand the term "within the veil" to apply? If the term "within the veil" applies to the first apartment, then we would expect that it had been thus applied so universally in the Old Testament Scriptures, that the reader would not hesitate in applying it to the first apartment. But when I came to study the matter carefully I found that the term "within the veil," in the Old Testament never applied to the place within the door of the tabernacle, or the first apartment, but always to the holy of holies, within the veil which separated the holy from the most holy. I found that the Hebrew Scriptures never call the curtain at the door of the tabernacle "a veil," much less "the veil." On the other hand, the term "veil" is applied to the curtain separating the holy from the most holy; and the term "within the veil" applies only to the holy of holies (Ballenger, 20, 21).

A close study of the Hebrew Bible and its translation into Greek, the Septuagint, reveals that the evidence isn't as clear-cut as Ballenger claims. While in general the linguistic data support his argument, he has overstated the case. For instance, in at least two places in the Hebrew Bible (Lev. 21:23; Num 18:7), the meaning of veil is open to question. Likewise, the Greek word for veil, *katapetasma*, in unqualified use refers at least once to the first curtain in the Septuagint (Ex. 26:37)—something that Ballenger asserts is never found. The actual phrase *within the veil* occurs only four times in the Septuagint and refers to the second curtain.

Ballenger's investigation of *within the veil* contains some valuable insights but ultimately is flawed. He diligently searched the Old Testament in an attempt to understand Hebrews 6:19, 20—but he failed to follow the argument of Hebrews itself! The first principle of interpretation calls upon the student to consider the context of the material he is studying. Hebrews 6:19, 20 only yields its meaning in light of the total discussion about Jesus' high-priestly ministry and sacrifice.

When we work through 8:1–10:18, we will see that the entire argumentation dealing with sacrifices, sanctuaries, and the Day of Atonement combines to portray the magnificence of Christianity—Jesus Christ, our High Priest, with a once-for-all, all-sufficient sacrifice. We will find that two great ideas emerge—finality and access: finality of sacrifice, because Christ's offering of Himself is complete and unrepeatable; and access, because by His death He has broken all barriers separating us from God and has thrown open the gates of heaven to everyone who believes in Him.

This is the big picture that Ballenger failed to perceive in Hebrews. He became so engrossed in a particular phrase, *within the veil*, and in concerns based on Old Testament types that he missed the message of Hebrews itself.

■ Applying the Word

Hebrews 4:14–6:20

1. **What does it mean that Jesus is a heavenly High Priest? How has my study of this chapter made that idea more attractive to me?**
2. **Do I approach "the throne of grace" confidently or fearfully? What does it mean to approach confidently? To approach fearfully? Do I feel that I *belong* in the heavenly courts? Why?**
3. **What is my spiritual maturity? Have I grown, or am I still an infant? What reasons can I give for my answer? Do I find the "solid food" of Hebrews palatable, or does it "turn me off"? Why?**
4. **How do the privileges of the Christian life that the Lord provides—the Holy Spirit, the Word of God, power—help me with my spiritual life?**
5. **A shocking question: What factors have the potential of**

changing me to the point that I would drift so far from the Lord as to publicly renounce Him? What can I do to safeguard against that happening?

6. Do I know anyone who once walked with Him but now seems utterly careless to spiritual things? What happened?

7. For me, what makes God's promises absolutely certain?

8. What anchors my life? Or—who? In what sense do I hold onto the anchor, and in what sense does it hold onto me?

■ Researching the Word

1. With the aide of a concordance, look up the occurrences of the word *grace* in Paul's epistles (Romans through Philemon). Make a list of the various ways Paul uses the word. Which of the uses in his other epistles comes closest to his use of the word in Hebrews 4:16? How do these other texts help you better understand what Paul means in 4:16?

2. Trace the biblical use of the phrase *within the veil*, using a concordance based on the King James Version. Read carefully the additional sources listed below on the problem. What special meaning does *within the veil* have for you in your relationship with Jesus?

3. Look up the word *priest* in the *SDA Bible Dictionary* (899-902). Identify the various changes in priesthood throughout history. Read about the change in priesthood in the New Testament era in 1 Peter 2:9. What is the difference between the priesthood of believers that Peter talks about and Christ's priesthood as Paul describes it in Hebrews 5:1-10 and 6:19, 20? What special contribution does each of these ideas make to our spiritual life as Christians?

■ Further Study of the Word

1. For a discussion of Jesus as High Priest, see W. G. Johnsson, *In Absolute Confidence*, 75-97; B. F. Westcott, *The Epistle to the Hebrews*, 137-141.

2. For the problem of 6:4-6, see F. F. Bruce, *The Epistle to the Hebrews*, rev. ed., 144-149.
3. For Ballenger and "within the veil," see W. G. Johnsson, "Day of Atonement Allusions," in *Issues in the Book of Hebrews*, 105-120, and A. V. Wallenkampf, "A Brief Review of Some of the Internal and External Challengers to the Seventh-day Adventist Teachings in the Sanctuary and the Atonement," in *The Sanctuary and the Atonement*, 582-603.

CHAPTER FIVE

The Better Priesthood

Hebrews 7

After a long exhortation, the apostle picks up the discussion where he left off at 5:10—Jesus "was designated by God to be high priest in the order of Melchizedek." As in 4:14–5:10, where he expounded the role of Jesus as High Priest, so now he will elaborate His better priesthood— one after the order of Melchizedek.

Hebrews 7 is arguably the least understood chapter of the entire Bible. When Christians want to illustrate the difficulties of Scripture, they commonly refer to verses from this passage, such as Melchizedek being without father or mother or beginning (7:3) or Levi not yet born but paying tithe to Melchizedek through Abraham (vss. 9, 10).

Still the chapter contains precious truth for the student of the Word. If we read it whole, not concentrating on its seemingly obscure verses, we will find here important ideas that shed much light on Jesus, our great High Priest. Tempting though it may be to skip or skim over this apparently uninviting chapter, I welcome you, reader, to an exciting study.

■ Getting Into the Word

Hebrews 7

Read Hebrews 7 straight through without trying to figure out difficult verses. Now study it again as part of the developing discussion about Jesus' high priesthood by reading 4:14–5:10, skipping 5:11–6:18, and starting again at 6:19

through to the summary at 8:1, 2. Finally, read 7:1-28 a third time. Does the chapter begin to emerge in clearer light? Here are some questions to aid you in your investigations:

1. With the aid of a concordance, look up the other references to Melchizedek in the Bible, and study them in context.
2. Who is the leading figure, the center of discussion in 7:1-28? Is the chapter really about Melchizedek?
3. Psalm 110:4 plays a key role in this chapter. List each time the apostle quotes from it and the point he makes.
4. Why is it important that Jesus be shown to be a priest according to a new order of priesthood?
5. Does "there must also be a change of the law" (vs.12) suggest that the Ten Commandments were abolished in the New Testament era? Explain your answer.
6. Notice the places where *perfection* or *perfect* occur in Hebrews 7. What does Paul have in mind by this terminology?
7. List the various points in which Hebrews 7 sets forth Jesus as a better High Priest than those of the Aaronic order.

■ Exploring the Word

Mystery Man!

The mysterious, shadowy figure of Melchizedek has fascinated Christians for many centuries. They have speculated concerning the description of 7:3: "Without father or mother, without genealogy, without beginning of days or end of life . . . he remains a priest forever." Some have suggested that Melchizedek was Christ, appearing on earth for the encounter with Abraham long before His birth in Bethlehem. Others have suggested that he was perhaps out of this world, a being from an unfallen planet.

And, yes—some Adventists have claimed that Ellen White revealed Melchizedek's identity in a secret testimony. I remember well meeting a man at dusk many years ago when I was a student at Avondale College in Australia. He had, he said, "something special" to show me, and he brought out a dog-eared piece of paper with a message purportedly from Mrs. White during the time when she lived at Avondale (1892-1900). The secret testimony?—Melchizedek was the Holy Spirit! (The Ellen G. White Estate considers that one, along with various others, to be apocryphal.)

Christians are not the only ones who have puzzled over Melchizedek. The rabbis had a field day trying to account for him. They, of course, didn't have to grapple with Hebrews 7:3, but they had the task of trying to fit this priest into the Old Testament scheme. For them, Abraham was the supreme figure of the Bible—father of the nation and father of faith. But in Genesis 14:18-20, a mysterious figure appears on the scene, one apparently greater than Abraham, because he blesses the patriarch. Further, long before Levi or Aaron, long before the Jewish priesthood, the Scriptures describe this man as already a priest.

One explanation argued that Melchizedek was Shem, the son of Noah. The genealogies allow for Shem and Abraham to be contemporaries, and this suggestion kept the Old Testament priesthood "in the family." Another speculation, even farther out, suggested that, because in Genesis 14:19, 20 Melchizedek blessed Abraham before he blessed God, God took the priesthood away from him!

Even among the people of Qumran, those sectarians who lived in the forbidding hills by the Dead Sea, we find speculation concerning Melchizedek. One of their scrolls, poorly preserved, tells of a ministry by Melchizedek in the heavenly sanctuary.

Truly, where the evidence is scant, theories multiply. But God hasn't left us to solve the riddle of Hebrews by mental gymnastics. When we read the chapter as a whole, considering its total thrust in the context of the entire book of Hebrews, two facts emerge that put all the speculation about Melchizedek in new light.

First, Christ, not Melchizedek, gives focus to the chapter. The author isn't concerned about Melchizedek, per se, but about Jesus. Melchizedek comes into the discussion only to the extent that he illuminates Jesus and His work.

We see this fact graphically demonstrated in 7:3. After the three verses summarizing the Old Testament meeting of Abraham and Melchizedek, Paul writes about the latter: *"Like the Son of God* he remains a priest forever." Since Melchizedek was chronologically prior to Jesus' incarnation, which constituted Him a priest, we might expect the concluding statement in 7:3 to read: "And the Son of God is like him." But Jesus, not Melchizedek, is the center, so Melchizedek is compared to Him instead.

All those efforts to figure out Melchizedek are, therefore, largely misdirected. We should concentrate on Jesus, not Melchizedek!

Second, the key Old Testament passage shaping the argument of Hebrews 7 is Psalm 110:4, not Genesis 14:18-20. The *order* of Melchizedek, rather than Melchizedek himself—this emerges as the crucial concern.

According to the Levitical order, Jesus could not be a priest, because He was born from the tribe of Judah. He was disqualified by birth. But now, Psalm 110:4 enters the picture: It is the one place in the Old Testament that arouses expectation of the rise of a new priestly order, one that will supersede the Levitical. So Jesus *can* be a priest—because the rules will change.

In fact, Psalm 110:4 not only provides the scriptural base for the reasoning of Hebrews 7, it impregnates the entire book. The apostle continually quotes it in full or in part or alludes to it. He finds it a rich theological source for the high-priestly ministry of Jesus:

1. In 5:6 the words of appointment are quoted in full to show that Christ is divinely designated as High Priest (even as was Aaron). In 5:10 he merely summarizes 5:6.
2. In 6:20 only the final part ("priest forever, in the order of Melchizedek") is quoted. By this means, the author picks up the thread dropped at 5:10 and also introduces the entire

discussion of chapter 7.

3. In 7:11 he alludes to Psalm 110:4, reasoning for the necessity of a new order of priesthood.

4. In 7:15, 17 the words of institution again are quoted in full. Here he contrasts the new order with the old one, which required physical descent from Levi.

5. In 7:20, 21 the stress falls on the first part of Psalm 110:4, with its divine oath: "The Lord has sworn and will not change his mind."

6. In 7:24 there is an allusion emphasizing the continuing high priesthood of Christ: "permanent priesthood."

7. In 7:28 there is a final allusion to Psalm 110:4, in which the motifs of high priest, oath, divine appointment, and eternal office come together.

We may set out the changing emphases in the allusions to Psalm 110:4 by underscoring the key words for each of the above instances.

1. 5:6—*priest* forever.
2. 6:20—the order of *Melchizedek.*
3. 7:11—the *order* of Melchizedek.
4. 7:15-17—the *order of Melchizedek.*
5. 7:20, 21—the Lord *has sworn.*
6. 7:24—*forever.*
7. 7:28—*forever.*

Puzzling Verses

The first 10 verses of Hebrews 7 argue one main idea: "Just think how great he [that is, Melchizedek] was!" He was not only greater than Abraham but greater than Levi. The implication, then, is that the order of Melchizedek is greater than the order of Levi.

In developing this idea, the apostle first reminds his readers about this mysterious figure from Israel's distant past. He takes the account of Genesis 14:18-20 and comments on it, not just summarizing it but treating it selectively. What he omits is as interesting as what he elaborates.

He makes no mention of the bread and wine that Melchizedek gave to Abraham. If Paul had wanted to allegorize, these items would certainly have provided a perfect opportunity to bring in the Lord's Supper, which Jesus, out Priest-King, makes available to us. A Jewish writer roughly contemporary with Paul, Philo Judaeus, showed what a fertile imagination could do with the story of Melchizedek: He saw in the wine the soul's intoxication with God!

But Paul isn't concerned with the Lord's Supper, so he passes over the bread and the wine. That also tells us that he does not see Jesus' sacrificial death as tied to these elements. Shortly—in chapters 9 and 10—he will take up the "better blood" that won our salvation, and, had he held to teaching like that of the mass, this would have been the place to prepare readers for it. He makes no such connection, however, and the silence is deafening!

Nor does he develop the royal aspect of Jesus. Although he makes the point that Melchizedek was both king and priest, he doesn't take it farther. *Melchizedek* means literally "king of righteousness," and since he was king in Salem (Jerusalem), which means "peace," he was also "king of peace."

Jesus as King of Righteousness and King of Peace provides a fruitful sermon topic. You won't find that sermon in Hebrews, however. The apostle nowhere comes back to these ideas. Although throughout the book we find Jesus assigned the prerogatives of royalty—as early as 1:3 we see Him seated at God's right hand in heaven—that aspect isn't the focus or concern of Hebrews.

Jesus as Priest rather than as King—this is where the interest lies. And that is why Melchizedek enters the discussion. This ancient person, who was a priest long before Aaron, sheds light on the ministry of our great High Priest.

Which brings us to Hebrews 7:3—"Without father or mother, without genealogy, without beginning of days or end of life, like the Son of God he remains a priest forever." After all the speculation for so many years about Melchizedek, the explanation is simple.

In commenting on Genesis 14:18-20, Paul used an approach common to his time in which the *silence* of the text, as well as its data, provides a basis for study. We have noticed what Genesis 14:18-20 tells us about Melchizedek; notice now what it *doesn't* tell us. We find no parents mentioned, no genealogy, no record of birth or death. According to the bare record, Melchizedek simply appears on the scene, as though he had never been born or never died, as though he were forever a priest.

Long-time editor of the *Review and Herald* Uriah Smith had it right a century ago. "Lastly, let it further be borne in mind that the expressions, which are to many so perplexing, are written from the standpoint of the record we have of Melchizedek, which gives us no particulars on these points," he wrote. "These expressions are: 'without father,' 'without mother,' 'having neither beginning of days, nor end of life,' 'of whom it is witnessed, that he liveth.' The record tells us nothing about his pedigree, his birth, or death. So far as the record goes, no beginning nor end of life is given; and it was the custom therefore, among the Jews, to speak of such as having no genealogy, no mother, no father, no beginning of days, nor end of life. And considering that all these expressions are used simply from the standpoint of the record, there is no difficulty. Melchizedek suddenly appears upon the scene of action, an eminent servant of God, combining in his own person the double office of king and priest. All before him is blank; all following him is blank. Neither birth nor death appearing in the scene, he becomes a fitting prototype of Christ in his position of priest-king in this dispensation" (*Review and Herald*, 5 Nov. 1895).

If the author of Hebrews were primarily involved in a treatise on Melchizedek, we would find this reasoning forced and artificial. But he isn't. As we noticed above on Hebrews 7:3, his focus is really on Jesus. Melchizedek—as he appears in the biblical record—is like Jesus. Jesus, on the other hand, is not like Melchizedek. (Notice how the subheading in the NIV following verse 10 misses the point: "Jesus Like Melchizedek"!)

Melchizedek and Levi

Hebrews 7:4-10 sets out the greatness of Melchizedek. Two acts establish his superiority over Abraham: The patriarch gave him a tithe of the plunder, and Melchizedek blessed Abraham. "Without doubt the lesser person is blessed by the greater" (vs. 7). But the apostle's interest runs beyond Abraham. Although most of the paragraph deals with the patriarch and Melchizedek, verses 9 and 10 show us where the argument is headed. Melchizedek is greater, not only than Abraham, but than Levi.

Observe how he reaches this conclusion: Levi "paid" tithe through his great-grandfather's act! Strange reasoning indeed! After we have struggled with verse 3, we now encounter this. No wonder that Hebrews 7 is notorious among Bible students! As with verse 3, however, a little prayerful reflection can break the impasse. Plus a little humility. We tend to set up our twentieth-century thought processes as superior. We think logic that doesn't flow in the Greco-Roman way of reasoning we inherited is foreign and flawed.

But does our age have all wisdom? Here is logic of a different kind, but logic that may have something important for us if we will take the time to enter it. And, we should remember, this is *biblical* logic, so we do well to put aside our feelings of superiority of knowledge and reasoning processes.

In fact, an idea that most people in the West have lost and that they need to recover lies back of Hebrews 7:9, 10. For generations, men and women have been nurtured on the philosophy of the individual, the one person, alone, solitary, before God and humanity. Individuality is important, but it is only half the picture. The Bible supplies the other half. It tells us that we are *more* than individuals. We have a corporate identity as well as an individual identity. We are part of each other. "No man is an island," as John Donne wrote, so the tolling of another's bell is the tolling of our death also. When one—anyone—suffers, hurts, or dies, we, too, are diminished.

We find the concept of corporate identity and personality

throughout the Scriptures—when we can break out of our modern, restricted mode of thinking and discern it. For instance, when Jesus confronted Saul on the Damascus road, He said, "Saul, Saul, why do you persecute me?" . . . "I am Jesus, whom you are persecuting" (Acts 9:4, 5). Now Saul had been harassing the followers of Jesus, not Jesus Himself—or so our individualistic mode tells us. But the Bible opens to us the corporate mode. Jesus and His followers are so bound together that to persecute Christians is to persecute their Lord.

The clearest and most important expressions of corporate identity occur in the key terms *in Adam* and *in Christ*. We all are "in" Adam—we are one people, one race, or sinners with one doom. But, praise God, Christ has made a new race of people with one eternal life. When He died, we died; when He rose, we rose also. So long as we choose to be His, we remain in Him.

"As in Adam all die, so in Christ all will be made alive." "Just as through the disobedience of the one man the many were made sinners, so also through the obedience of the one man the many will be made righteous." "If we have been united with him in his death, we will certainly also be united with him in his resurrection" (1 Cor. 15:22; Rom. 5:19; 6:5).

We are part of each other; we belong to one another—this concept, taken seriously, could transform society and church. We'd realize that we are more than a Social Security number, a nameless face in the crowd. We'd have less need for group-therapy sessions. We'd begin to look out for each other. And the church would become more accepting of and caring for broken men and women.

So Hebrews 7:9, 10 makes a lot of sense for our times. In terms of the apostle's argument, it enables him to show that Melchizedek is greater than Levi, because Levi, progenitor of those appointed to receive tithes, "paid" tithe to Melchizedek.

Verse 8 introduces another point. Melchizedek "is declared to be living"—that is, the record does not mention his death. So "he remains a priest forever" (vs. 3). The apostle will draw out the implications of this idea when he lays out the superiority of Jesus' priestly order later in the chapter.

The Rise of a New Priesthood

The next paragraph, 7:11, 19, shows where the discussion of the first ten verses is headed. "It is clear," writes the author, "that our Lord descended from Judah, and in regard to that tribe Moses said nothing about priests" (vs. 14). The first and prime concern, then, is to establish that Jesus *can* be a priest, even though He wasn't born into the priestly tribe, the Levites.

To many of us today, that point may seem hardly worth all the reasoning of chapter 7. We may be sure, however, that the matter wasn't a small one to the original readers (and, incidentally, provides further support for their being Jewish Christians). The claim for Jesus' high priesthood must have fallen strangely, even offensively, on first-century ears, especially while the temple in Jerusalem still stood, as it did up to A.D. 70, with its sacrificial services. Not only Jews but also Christians demanded evidence for such an assertion.

According to the Old Testament law, Jesus did not qualify for the priesthood. But Scripture itself predicted that a new order of priesthood would arise and that God would designate One as Priest of the new order. "You are a priest forever, in the order of Melchizedek" (vs. 17). So Jesus, born of Judah's line, becomes priest by God's proclamation, which changes ancient ways and structures.

The argument goes farther, however. Not only can Jesus *be* a priest, He is a *better* priest. Hebrews 7:1-10 "proves" that Melchizedek is superior to Abraham and hence, to Levi, so the Melchizedekian order surpasses the old one. This is the intent of the "and what we have said is even more clear" in 7:15. The new Priest, Jesus, hasn't come to office "on the basis of a regulation as to his ancestry but on the basis of the power of an indestructible life" (vs. 16). Here, Paul pulls together hints that we saw in two places earlier in the chapter: "Without beginning of days or end of life, like the Son of God he remains a priest forever" (vs. 3) and "him who is declared to be living" (vs. 8).

The remainder of chapter 7 will lay out specific ways in which the new order surpasses the old. Before we look at them, however, two other items from 7:11-19 call for comment. Both are of particular interest to Seventh-day Adventists.

In verse 12 the apostle speaks about "a change of the law." Occasionally, one will find antinomians referring to this text for support—occasionally, but not frequently, because anyone who looks at the context will see the fallacy of that approach. That the apostle refers to the regulations concerning the old order (that is, one had to be *born* of the tribe of Levi) and not the Ten Commandments is manifest from what he says in verses 12 to 16. He has in mind "a change of the priesthood" (vs. 12), and therefore, a corresponding change in the rules that determine who can be a priest.

The second item takes us back to the matter of perfection, which we noticed already in chapters 2 and 5. There, we saw this term applied to the Son, who was "perfected" by a series of human experiences—that is, He became qualified to be our great High Priest. In Hebrews 7 we find the terminology in a different context, now used with reference to the Levitical priesthood itself.

Hebrews 7:11 denies that perfection was possible under the older order. ("*If* perfection could have been attained through the Levitical priesthood.") The author repeats that thought in verses 18 and 19, calling the "former regulation" "weak and useless" and then stating flat-footedly, "For the law [the old law of the priesthood] made nothing perfect."

With this terminology, the apostle is preparing his reader for the long theological discussion of Christ's sacrifice that is about to follow. We will find the language of perfection again there and will withhold thorough study of it until we come to that section. Suffice it for us to notice at this point the clue to what is to follow. After a categorical statement of the deficiencies of the old order in 7:18, 19, Paul mentions a "better hope . . . *by which we draw near to God*." That idea—access to the Majesty of heaven—will emerge as a key element of the perfection that Jesus' new priestly order brings.

To this point in Hebrews 7, then, we see three ways in which the new order surpasses the old:

1. Melchizedek was greater than Levi, and so the Melchizedekian order is better than the Levitical.
2. The Melchizedekian order centers in "the power of an indestructible life" (vs. 16), but the Levitical, in "men who die" (vs. 8).
3. The Levitical order could not bring perfection, but the new order, which is better, presumably can—and Hebrews 8 to 10 will show that it does.

The Superiority of the New Priesthood

In the last part of Hebrews 7, verses 20-28, the author hammers home the superiority of Christ's priesthood. Here we find four new reasons advanced:

1. Christ became a priest with a divine oath (that is, Psalm 110:4), whereas the Levitical priests were simply given office by reason of the accident of birth into a particular tribe.

God's oath does more than confirm the fact of Christ's priesthood. It suggests direct intervention and involvement. Further, it removes any shadow of a doubt, making God's purpose very clear, as Hebrews 6:17 already told us in a different context.

No matter, then, if some *people* might challenge Christ's claim to be a priest—*God* has spoken! No matter if Jewish critics rise up to reject that claim—*God* has confirmed the fact by swearing an oath.

In our day, also, the teaching of our great High Priest sounds strange to many, remote from our world of computers and hitech. Regardless of our perspective or appreciation, however, that teaching stands steadfast, immovable, indestructible. The eternal God has spoken—indeed, has sworn an oath—and we may rest our confidence in His word.

2. Because Jesus lives forever, He has a permanent priesthood. His service is continuous, unbroken by succession, secure against death. Instead of many Levitical priests, now we have one Priest.

That truth carries important spiritual freight for us. It means we can always know who is minding the heavenly shop, who is in charge. We can know whom we are dealing with and what He is like. We know that we will always be accepted and always be welcome.

We read the New Testament, and we catch the throb of new life, new assurance, new hope pulsating through every page. God has come down to be among us, one of us! He has revealed Himself! He has dealt with our terrible sin problem, taking it on Himself, dying on our behalf. He has risen from the dead! And He will come back to receive us to Himself.

Too often in our times, the fizz has gone out of Christian living. We wander about, groping for a light, when the Light has already come. We debate and argue, when the Truth already has spoken. We seek to please God, when He already has opened the Way.

One Saviour, one Lord, one Priest—this is what Hebrews 7 affirms. He is the same for us as He was for Paul and Peter and John. His ministry goes on, never ceasing, in the heavenly courts. Always He intercedes for us (not that the Father is unwilling to hear). Always He hears our heart cry. Always He saves—and saves completely.

3. Our great High Priest provides the solution to the sin problem; He is not a part of it. Under the old order, the high priests needed to offer sacrifices, not only for the people, but for themselves as well. They were part of the problem they were trying to deal with.

But not Jesus! No such need for Him—He is the high priest from *outside* the system. Just as He didn't become a priest according to the old regulations, so He wasn't a part of the old system. He is "holy, blameless, pure, set apart from sinners, exalted above the heavens" (vs. 26).

"Such a high priest," says the apostle, "meets our need." How true! We need someone who can break the cycle of sin and sacrifice, someone to show us a better way, someone not part of the establishment.

Jesus was without sin. He was, as 7:26 tells us, "set apart from sinners." Let us never forget it, never suggest or imply that He was just like us. Like us in shared experiences of suffering, testing, and submission to the divine will—yes; but radically different from us in that He needed no sacrifice, no forgiveness.

Ellen White, who encourages us to study the humanity of Jesus, calling it "a fruitful field," also warns us against any tendency to make Him just like us:

> The humanity of the Son of God is everything to us. It is the golden chain that binds our souls to Christ, and through Christ to God. This is to be our study. *Christ was a real man*; he gave proof of his humility in becoming a man. *Yet he was God in the flesh*. When we approach this subject, we would do well to heed the words spoken by Christ to Moses at the burning bush, "Put off thy shoes from off thy feet, for the place whereon thou standest is holy ground." We should come to this study with the humility of a learner, with a contrite heart. And the study of the incarnation of Christ is a fruitful field, which will repay the searcher who digs deep for hidden truth ("Search the Scriptures," *The Youth's Instructor*, 13 Oct. 1898, emphasis supplied).

Praise God for this holy High Priest, One so like us but also so unlike us, who alone can meet our needs!

4. Finally—and this is the climactic word—at the head of the new priesthood stands the perfected Son (vs. 28). The Levitical order, even in its purest manifestation, could never approach this mark. That term *Son* carries the weight of full deity, as we saw in studying Hebrews 1.

And *perfected* Son opens up the range of His life on earth as He learned what it means to be human, but throughout remained in touch with the Father and free from sin, as we saw in Hebrews 2 and 5.

What a priest!

Again we notice how the author, following his customary mastery of development, lays the ground for the discussion to follow.

Toward the end of the chapter, he simply drops the term *better covenant* (verse 22). That theme, however, becomes central to the next section of the book (8:1–9:15).

■ Applying the Word

Hebrews 7

1. Which aspect of Jesus' priesthood mentioned in Hebrews 7 do I find especially nurtures my spiritual life? Which aspect gives me the greatest hope and assurance?
2. How can I take the great ideas of this chapter and find meaning for my life today? For instance, how does the teaching of corporate identity that is shown in the discussion of 7:4-10 apply to the way I see myself and other people?
3. To what extent was it necessary that Jesus be exactly like me in order to leave me an example? To what extent was it necessary that He partake of every human experience? How does His participation in suffering, temptation, and death help me?
4. Think of experiences that Jesus did not, and could not, have shared—for instance, those unique to women, to married people, or to modern times. How does the apostle's instruction in Hebrews thus far help me better understand—and explain—the tension between His likeness to us and His differences from us?
5. When I give my word, how sure is it? Can others count on it? When have I kept my word, even though doing so hurt? Why did I do that? Have there been times when I did not keep my word? Why?
6. In what ways does Jesus seem more real to me after studying Hebrews 7? Which passages in this chapter especially strengthen my assurance of His unfailing willingness to help me? What special assurance do I gain from each one?

■ Researching the Word

1. Use a concordance to look up the words *Levi* and *Levites* in the first five books of the Bible. Why was the tribe of Levi given the priesthood? Who was the first high priest from the tribe of Levi? Even though Christ is not from the tribe of Levi, what character traits of the Levites does He have that qualify Him to be a priest?
2. Look up the references in Hebrews to Christ's temptations and His having been made perfect (2:10, 17, 18; 4:15; 5:9; 7:28). Next, read the story of Christ's trial from at least one of the Gospels. Begin with Gethsemene, and read through to His crucifixion. In what sense do you think this experience contributed to His perfection? How can trials contribute to your perfection?

■ Further Study of the Word

1. For a better understanding of the methods of interpreting the Old Testament that were used by the Jewish expositors of Paul's day, and to identify which ones we find in Hebrews 7:1-3, see P. E. Hughes, *A Commentary on the Epistle to the Hebrews*, 237-250.
2. For a straightforward exegesis of each verse of Hebrews 7, see F. F. Bruce, *The Epistle to the Hebrews*, rev. ed., 156-179.
3. For a scholarly exegesis of Hebrews 7 with detailed reference to the Greek text, see B. F. Westcott, *The Epistle to the Hebrews*, 170-210.

PART THREE

The Magnificence
of Jesus' Work

Hebrews 8:1–10:18

CHAPTER SIX

The Better Covenant

Hebrews 8:1–9:10

We have now arrived at the summit of the theological development of Hebrews. The discussion moves from the person to the work of Christ, and, in a sustained passage of close reasoning and deep power, the apostle will unpack the meaning of that phrase from the overture to the book— "He [Christ] . . . provided purification for sins" (1:3).

This section, 8:1–10:18, forges relentlessly forward without pause for exhortation, and we conceivably could study it in one big bite. But because of its length, we will divide it into two chapters, building our treatment around the two ideas that, while running through the entire section, tend to dominate each half—"covenant" for 8:1–9:10 and "blood" for 9:11–10:18.

■ Getting Into the Word

Hebrews 8:1–9:10

Read 8:1–10:18 from the New International Version at one sitting, watching for the main themes that emerge and trying to follow the apostle's logical development. Disregard chapter breaks. Then do the same reading from a different translation. Finally, go back to the NIV and read 8:1–9:10 slowly and carefully. After this concentrated, prayerful study, try answering the following questions:

1. List the evidences pointing to a heavenly sanctuary.
2. Study the relationship between the earthly and heavenly sanctuaries as revealed by this passage. What details do you find concerning the heavenly?
3. With a concordance, look up all the occurrences of *covenant* in Hebrews, noting contexts and accompanying adjectives such as *new, first,* or *eternal.*
4. Hebrews 8:8-12 contains the longest Old Testament quotation in the entire New Testament. What point or points does Paul make from this quotation?
5. Examine carefully the uses of *sanctuary* and *tabernacle* in 8:1–10:18. In two columns, list each reference with the terms used by the New International Version. In a third column, list the terms used in these verses by the Revised Standard Version. In a fourth column, list the terms used by the King James Version in these verses.
6. Notice the description of the earthly sanctuary in 9:1-5. Do you find anything surprising here? Compare the passage with Exodus 25:10–27:19.
7. What limitations or inadequacies of the old system emerge in Hebrews 9:6-10?

■ Exploring the Word

The Heavenly Sanctuary—the Genuine One

The passage commences on a note of high confidence. Summing up the discussion of the previous four chapters, the apostle gives their "point," or "pith," as Coverdale, an early English translator, rendered the Greek: "We *do* have such a high priest." Notice Coverdales note of certainty.

From the standpoint of the people of His time, Jesus was anything but a high priest. A poor man from the tribe of Judah, a Galilean, a provincial, unlearned in the rabbinical schools, outside the political system that manipulated the sacerdotal office, He seemed the unlikeliest person to embody such a claim. But the assertion was true because He was God's Man, designated by the Father to be High Priest.

The entire book rings with such unequivocal affirmations. "*He is able* to help those who are being tempted," we read (2:18). And, "*We have* a great high priest who has gone through the heavens" (4:14); "*he is able* to save completely those who come to God through him" (7:25); "*we have* confidence to enter the Most Holy Place" (10:19); "*we have* an altar" (13:10). Christian assurance, the apostle is saying, rests on fact, on eternal realities in the heavens. It does not rest on feelings or impressions, either on hope or even promise, but on what already *is*.

In several places the apostle sets out the superiority of the heavenly sanctuary. He calls it "the true tabernacle" (8:2), of which the earthly sanctuary was but a "copy" and "shadow" (vs. 5). In 9:11 it is "the greater and more perfect tabernacle that is not man-made, that is to say, not a part of this creation." He reverts to "copies" for the earthly at 9:23 and again at 9:24—"a man-made sanctuary that was only a copy of the true one." But he then goes on to call the better sanctuary "heaven itself."

It is clear that Paul both compares and contrasts the earthly and heavenly sanctuaries. While Moses made everything according to the pattern God showed him on Mount Sinai (Exod. 25:40), that pattern was a blueprint for the work he was about to do, not of the heavenly reality. No human structure could duplicate the dwelling place of God; at best, it could only point to that perfect temple.

> The matchless splendor of the earthly tabernacle reflected to human vision the glories of that heavenly temple where Christ our forerunner ministers for us before the throne of God. The abiding place of the King of kings, where thousand thousands minister unto Him, and ten thousand times ten thousand stand before Him (Daniel 7:10); that temple, filled with the glory of the eternal throne, where seraphim, its shining guardians, veil their faces in adoration, could find, in the most

magnificent structure ever reared by human hands, but
a faint reflection of its vastness and glory (White, *The
Great Controversy, 414*).

But the earthly sanctuary prefigured the work of the heavenly
sanctuary. All its parts, furniture, and ritual pointed forward to
One who would fulfill the earthly and surpass it. We may speak of
correspondence between the two sanctuaries, to type and antitype,
of shadow and reality, but never of replication, for the heavenly,
where Christ ministers as both Priest and Sacrifice, could not be
conceived or made on a human scale.

A further matter of vital importance to interpreting Hebrews
has engaged students of the book for many years. As we examine
the language Paul used to describe the heavenly sanctuary in relation to the earthly, we find that it is very similar to the terminology used by Philo Judaeus. This writer, a Jew influenced by
Hellenistic thought who lived from about 20 B.C. to A.D. 50,
wrote about a heavenly sanctuary but in allegorical fashion. Philo,
like Plato before him, set out a two-level cosmology, with things
on earth as shadows or copies of heavenly archetypes. For Philo,
the heavenly sanctuary was the universe.

Noting the close affinities of expression between Philo and Hebrews, many scholars have held, and continue to hold, that we
should understand all the discussion in Hebrews about Christ's
priestly work in the heavenly sanctuary as setting out great truths
but not pointing to a specific ministry in an actual heavenly temple.

Careful consideration of the argument of Hebrews 8:1–10:18,
however, leads us to reject this interpretation. While Hebrews
indeed shows similarities to Philo's ideas, we find major differences of conception. In Hebrews, the heavenly realities do not
stand over against the earthly copies or shadows in eternal con-
tradistinction—they are crossed by time. For Hebrews, events in
time, events on earth, impact on events in heaven in a manner
that Philo, and Plato before him, would not have accepted.

Thus, Christ has not been High Priest in the heavenly tabernacle for all eternity. Rather, He became High Priest because of

the experiences He went through as a human being on this earth two thousand years ago. Nor does He offer an eternal sacrifice. He offered Himself once for all, and on earth, as He yielded His life on Calvary. Hebrews 10:1 shows sharply how in Hebrews, the vertical, spacial scheme of Philo is crossed by a linear, temporal one: "The law is only a shadow of the good things that are coming—not the realities themselves."

In recent years biblical scholarship has begun to swing away from the Philonic interpretation of Hebrews. Several Jewish writings from the last two centuries before Christ indicate belief in an actual heavenly sanctuary with angels as ministers. The Dead Sea Scrolls have underscored the point. One scroll, although poorly preserved, seems to indicate belief in Melchizedek mediating in the heavenly sanctuary. Many scholars today, therefore, assert that Hebrews should be understood against a background of apocalyptic Judaism rather than from Philo's writings.

Thus, the long-standing Adventist interpretation that holds to an actual ministry of Christ in an actual heavenly temple finds increasing support. Further, archaeological discoveries help us grasp why Paul went to such lengths in chapter 1 to show that the Son is greater than angels and why he used Melchizedek in chapter 7 to argue for Jesus' superior high-priestly office.

Tent, Sanctuary, and Places

Adventists' interest in the sanctuary language of Hebrews extends beyond the discussion above. We are largely alone among modern Christians in our emphasis on the heavenly ministry of Jesus, and, further, we understand that this ministry falls into two distinct phases. We believe His mediatorial work corresponded to the priestly functions of the earthly sanctuary that took place in the first apartment and lasted up to 1844. Since 1844, He has engaged in a second-apartment work, to which the activities of the Old Testament Day of Atonement pointed.

Understandably, Hebrews has been of key Adventist concern since the days of our pioneers. They understood that the 2,300-

day prophecy of Daniel 8:14, with its declaration of the eventual cleansing of the sanctuary, pointed to the work of Christ in heaven that commenced in 1844. Since the book of Hebrews is the one New Testament document that systematically builds on Leviticus and the sanctuary, early Adventists looked to this book for specific information about events in the heavenly sanctuary.

The student of Hebrews today finds surprising differences among the translations for the sanctuary terminology. These variations probably don't trouble the average reader, but they are of vital concern to Adventists, given our prophetic understanding. We must therefore probe this matter in some depth, even though it will mean going back to the Greek text.

The term with which we must wrestle is *ta hagia*, which, with its variants, occurs a total of ten times in the New Testament, all of them in Hebrews. *Ta hagia* is neuter plural and means literally "the holy things" or "the holy places." As we list the ten occurrences of this term and variants with translations from the New International Version, Revised Standard Version, and King James Version, we begin to see the difficulties Adventists, in particular, face:

Reference	Greek	NIV	KJV	RSV
8:2	*tōn hagiōn*	sanctuary	sanctuary	sanctuary
9:1	*to te hagiōn*	sanctuary	sanctuary	sanctuary
9:2	*hagia*	Holy Place	sanctuary	Holy Place
9:3	*hagia hagiōn*	Most Holy Place	Holiest of all	Holy of Holies
9:8	*tōn hagiōn*	Most Holy Place	holiest of all	sanctuary
9:12	*ta hagia*	Most Holy Place	holy place	Holy Place
9:24	*hagia*	sanctuary	holy places	sanctuary
9:25	*ta hagia*	Most Holy Place	holy place	Holy Place
10:19	*tōn hagiōn*	Most Holy Place	holiest	sanctuary
13:11	*ta hagia*	Most Holy Place	sanctuary	sanctuary

The differences are pronounced in four places: In 9:8, where the New International Version translates as "Most Holy Place," the King James Version has "holiest of all" and the Revised Standard Version has "sanctuary." In 9:12, where the New International Version has "Most Holy Pace," the King James Version has "holy place," and the Revised Standard Version has "Holy Place." In 9:25, where the New International Version reads "Most Holy Place," the King James Version has "holy place," and the Revised Standard Version has "Holy Place." Finally, in 10:19, where the New International Version has "Most Holy Place," the King James Version has "holiest," and the Revised Standard Version has "sanctuary." And the wider the range of translations, the greater the variations (see Salom, "*Ta Hagia* in the Epistle to the Hebrews").

We might think that the Septuagint (the Hebrew Old Testament translated into Greek) would help us solve the mystery of *ta hagia*. The term appears 170 times with reference to the tabernacle or temple, but it shows significant variations in form and application. While the majority of uses (142) refer to the sanctuary in general, in nineteen places it refers to the Holy Place and in nine to the Most Holy Place. As in the book of Hebrews, the Septuagint uses the term in both plural (the majority) and singular form, and both with and without the definite article. No consistent pattern can be found in these uses—the Septuagint shows a fluidity between plural and singular that mitigates against hard-and-fast conclusions. While we can say that the great majority of uses refer to the sanctuary in general, only the context can decide each particular case (Salom, 221).

That must be our approach in the book of Hebrews also. Where the apostle's reasoning clearly indicates that he is referring to a particular apartment, we can feel free to designate *ta hagia* or its variants by "Holy Place" or "Most Holy Place." However, where the context leaves his meaning uncertain, we will be wise to translate merely as "sanctuary."

This calls for a word about the New International Version. I think this is, in general, an excellent translation, but I disagree with its approach in Hebrews. The translators, in most cases, render *ta hagia* as "Most Holy Place," even where the context leaves the apostle's meaning in doubt. In my judgment they would have been fairer with the reader by translating the uncertain references

by the more neutral "sanctuary." The upshot is that all students of
Hebrews, and especially Adventists, need to be discriminating and
ready to challenge the New International Version wherever they
find "Most Holy Place." They should carefully examine the context and decide whether designation of a specific apartment is justified.

We will study each occurrence of *ta hagia* as we come to it. The
first five come in 8:1–9:10 and, with the exception of the fifth, are
clear-cut. As illustrations of the principle that the context must
decide the translation, we will take up the first four uses here.

In 8:2, the apostle calls Christ a high priest "who serves in *tōn
hagiōn*" (genitive case of *ta hagia*). The expression itself does not
occur in 8:5. Here, it is "a copy and shadow of the heavenly things,"
which the New International Version reasonably translates as "a
sanctuary that is a copy and shadow of what is in heaven." The
total context of 8:1-6, contrasting the earthly priests and their
sanctuary with Christ and His sanctuary, points to *tōn hagiōn* in
8:2 as referring to the sanctuary in general rather than to a particular apartment.

In 9:1, the context again points to "sanctuary" as the translation, even though the form has changed from the plural in 8:2 to
the singular. Again the context is decisive. The paragraph 9:1-5
describes the apartments and furniture of the earthly sanctuary,
so 9:1 designates the whole structure rather than one part.

Hagia in 9:2 must refer to the Holy Place, since it contains the
lampstand, the table, and the consecrated bread. Likewise in 9:3,
hagia hagiōn refers to the Most Holy Place, because it lay behind
the second curtain and contained the ark of the covenant, the stone
tablets, and the cherubim (vss. 4, 5).

Thus, despite the variations in *ta hagia*, we are left in no doubt
as to Paul's meaning. The occurrence in 9:8 is not as clear, however, and we will look at this later in the chapter after we have
followed the argument that leads up to it.

A final word concerning *ta hagia* in general. The attempt to
find a consistent translation by seeking parallels with the uses of
tabernacle does not prove fruitful. The Greek for tabernacle is *skēnē*,

literally "tent"; but, like *ta hagia*, we find the word used for the whole sanctuary as well as for specific apartments.

In 8:2, for instance, *sanctuary* and *true tabernacle* are equivalent. We find a similar parallel in 9:1, 2. However, the New International Version translates 9:3 as, "Behind the second curtain was a *room* called the Most Holy Place," and again, it says in 9:6, 7 "the outer room" and "the inner room." The Greek literally reads "the first tent" and "the second" ("tent" understood). The word *skēnē* appears more frequently in the Greek text than the reader of the New International Version will realize. These occurrences, however, do not, in themselves, provide the key to translating *ta hagia*.

The New Covenant

Hebrews 8:6-13 introduces the new covenant, which, Paul tells us, is superior to the old one (vs. 6). Covenant is one of the great biblical concepts and is arguably the central motif of the Old Testament. The word basically means "contract" or "agreement," but in its biblical context, it contains rich meaning. It describes Yahweh's gracious approach to humanity, His going out to us and entering into relation with us in our fallen state in order that we might know Him and experience the power of His salvation and the abundance of His blessings.

In modern parlance, covenant means God coming to us and saying, "Let's make a deal." He takes the initiative; He makes the offer. We bring nothing to the table; He brings everything. We start from ground zero in negotiations; He starts from infinity. But He comes, nevertheless; He comes and offers. Of course, biblical covenant far surpasses human contracts, in which the parties are essentially equals, each with interests and demands. When Yahweh enters into covenant with humanity, He lays down the stipulations. We do not bargain with Him. Salvation and the covenant blessings must always come on His terms, never on ours.

Yet we have a part to play. We may refuse the divine offer, slight the gracious initiative, or we may gladly accept and enter the covenant, committing ourselves to the divine stipulations and in turn receiving the divine promises.

Divine condescension—this lies at the heart of biblical covenant. The Holy One binding Himself by oath to puny men and women. And so—a foreshadowing of that infinite condescension when God became man, taking human flesh, and pitching His tent among us as our Brother (John 1:14).

As fruitful as the topic of covenant is for study and spiritual nurture, it has nonetheless sparked controversy over the years. Some Christians have argued that the "old" covenant—the one Yahweh made with Israel at Sinai—was legalistic. Thereby, they have sought to disparage the keeping of the Ten Commandments.

Seventh-day Adventists have also argued over the "old" and "new" covenants. Some have maintained that the covenant made at Sinai was flawed because it rested on obedience rather than faith. Others have held that the covenant itself wasn't flawed, that, in fact, God has always had the same covenant, which He has restated to individuals and to Israel at various times. Thus the problem at Sinai wasn't with the covenant, per se, they say, but with the people.

We must lay aside these dogmatic agendas as we come to the text of Hebrews. Our primary task is to study covenant in the context of Hebrews and then to attempt to relate what we have found to the broader questions about covenant.

The first mention of covenant, the Greek *diathēkē*, is in Hebrews 7:22. Because of the divine oath constituting Jesus a priest in the order of Melchizedek, we are told, He has become the guarantor, or surety, of a better covenant. Although the apostle doesn't elaborate, we should note the direction in which he has pointed us: He links covenant with priesthood.

Chapter 8 underscores Jesus' better ministry: He serves in a better temple—the true one (8:1, 2)—and He has a better ministry than the levitical priests insofar as the covenant He mediates is superior to the old one (8:6). And this covenant is founded on better promises. What are these promises—God's or the people's? The ensuing discussion about covenant, which is concentrated in 8:6–9:11 but extends to 10:18, will reveal the answer.

Hebrews 8:7, 8, as it reads in the New International Version, shows a fine balance of ideas. In verse 7 we find that the "first" covenant was "wrong" or faulty; however, verse 8 tells us that "God found fault *with the people*." These verses, then, would support the view that the covenant itself at Sinai was flawless—the Israelites "blew" it.

Not so fast! The Greek text of verse 8 is ambiguous. As the footnote to the verse tells us, some ancient manuscripts read: "But *God found fault* and said to the people." Under this understanding, the covenant itself was faulty and not merely the people. So we must go farther to get to the bottom of this discussion.

The long quotation in Hebrews 8:8-12—the longest of any in the New Testament—contains several discrete ideas. We read of the prediction of a new covenant, Israel's failure long ago, the law of God put within the heart, no need for teachers as God will teach each person directly, and the forgiveness of sins. However, in the subsequent references to this quotation, we do not find elaboration of these various ideas. The author does not take them up and apply them, as he did earlier with Psalm 110:4 and Psalm 95:7-11. We find his intent with this quotation of Jeremiah 31:31-34 only by noting his subsequent references to covenant.

His immediate comment on the "first" covenant is that it has become obsolete. God's bringing forward the new renders it passé—it must disappear (8:13).

Immediately following, however, his reasoning takes a significant turn. "Now the first covenant had regulations for worship and also an earthly sanctuary," he tells us (9:1), and proceeds with a thumbnail description of the Mosaic sanctuary and its services (vss. 2-7). That is, he associates the first covenant with Israel's cultus—the sacrificial system.

The next set of references to covenant comes at 9:15-22. These verses call for close scrutiny later—the word translated "will" in the New International Version at 9:16, 17 is *diathēkē*, the same word for covenant. At this point, we will merely note that once again, the apostle links covenant with sacrifice—the first covenant being ratified by the blood of animals but the new by the blood of

Christ, which sets people free "from the sins committed under the first covenant" (9:15).

We find the final reference to covenant in 10:15-18. Here the author's line of thought, which has progressed steadily from 8:1, reaches a climax, and here we see at last his main point with regard to covenant. Returning to the citation from Jeremiah, he quotes only part of it—the forgiveness of sins. So that was his chief concern all along. With all the good things that the new covenant brings, its main benefit lies in providing a solution to the sin problem.

Covenant and cultus (the sacrificial system) intertwine in the apostle's thought. From his first mention of covenant, every reference, whether to the first covenant or the new, links with the sacrificial system:

- 7:22—Because of the divine oath constituting Jesus as High Priest, He becomes guarantor of a better covenant.
- 8:6—Jesus' better (that is, heavenly) ministry links with the better covenant He mediates.
- 8:7-13—The discussion of the new covenant in contrast with the old comes to focus in the ability of the new to provide forgiveness of sins.
- 9:1—The first covenant "had" the Mosaic sanctuary and sacrificial system.
- 9:15-22—Each covenant—the first and the new—had corresponding sacrifices—animals or Christ's own self. But only His sacrifice and the new covenant can provide forgiveness of sins.
- 10:15-18—Under the new covenant, as God predicted in Jeremiah 31:31-34, He would deal decisively with sins, so "there is no longer any sacrifice for sins."

Thus, the discussion about covenant in the book of Hebrews does not turn on the issue of legalism or grace. The two covenants here stand for two phases in the working out of God's purposes. The first phase was associated with the Old Testament sanctuary, with its human priesthood and its animal sacrifices. Despite all the ritual, despite adherence to the divine regulations, and despite so much slaughter of animals, this covenant could not provide a permanent answer to the sin problem. But God promised a new covenant in which one High Priest, Jesus Christ our Lord, ministers in the heavenly sanctuary and where He offers His own blood as sacrifice. Here is God taking upon Himself our woe and our despair. And here at last is the solution to our desperate need.

We should also note the three other occurrences of covenant in Hebrews. In 10:29 the author, speaking of Jesus, mentions "the blood of the covenant that sanctified him." Toward the close of the book, he refers in passing to "Jesus the mediator of a new covenant, and to the sprinkled blood that speaks a better word than the blood of Abel" (12:24). Then, in the benediction that closes out his sermon, he speaks of "the blood of the eternal covenant" (13:20).

Each of these occurrences happens incidentally. The sustained theological argument about Jesus' person and work has already concluded. But interestingly, in each case, covenant is in the context of blood, thus confirming our conclusion above about the linking of covenant with sacrifice.

We see, then, that the theology of covenant takes quite a different turn in Hebrews. It stands in sharp contrast to the allegory of the two covenants in Galatians 4:21-31, which oppose grace and legalism. However, the discussion in Hebrews complements, rather than contradicts, the Galatians presentation.

With this understanding of covenant in Hebrews, we can return to the question of the "better promises" of 8:6. They are better because they come from God, not men and women, and because they ensure the decisive removal of sin.

So where was the failure in the first covenant—with the covenant itself or with the people? The answer must be: both. The Israelites indeed fell short of Yahweh's intent for them—their promises were ropes of sand. But the old covenant was itself flawed—not that it was bad (after all, God set it up!), but that it, *in itself*, could never provide the decisive answer to the problem of human sin. In was valuable, but only for a time; if humankind was ever to be freed from sin, a new way and a new hope must come— not from humans, not from animal sacrifices, but from God Himself.

Two items remain as we wrap up our consideration of Hebrews 8:1–9:10. Both concern the author's presentation in chapter 9:1-10.

Limitations of the First Covenant

Hebrews 9:1-10 falls into two distinct paragraphs—the first five verses give a thumbnail description of the Old Testament sanctuary, and the second five point out the limitations of the old system.

The author bases his discussion on the portable sanctuary that Moses constructed according to the divine plan. It was not based on Solomon's temple, nor was it based on the later temple built after the Jews returned from captivity, which was refurbished by Herod the Great. We know this because Paul refers to "tents" several times (vss. 2, 3, 6-8). The NIV obscures his meaning, however. It translates the word for *tent* (the Greek *skēnē)* by "tabernacle" in verses 2, 8 but by "room" in verses 3, 6, 7. This point comes with heightened interest, if, as we suggested in the introduction to Hebrews, the second temple was still in use at the time of writing. It means that the apostle bypassed what was out there, the current center of Jewish worship, which was known to the world. Instead, he reasoned from the Old Testament scriptures *about* the sanctuary.

His account of the Mosaic sanctuary cuts to the bone and highlights its two main features—the Holy Place and the Most Holy Place. He shows no interest in attaching spiritual meaning or application to the various items of furniture in each of the two apartments. Many writers on the sanctuary, especially Adventists, have drawn valuable lessons as they have related each item of the sanctuary to Christ and His work, but the author of Hebrews cuts short any such consideration with the words "We cannot discuss these things in detail now" (vs. 5).

One item of his brief description in 9:15 surprises us. He places the altar of incense "behind the second curtain" in the Most Holy Place along with the ark of the covenant (vss. 3, 4). God's instructions to Moses called for this golden altar to be put in the Holy Place—"in front of the curtain" (Exod. 26:31-35; 30:1-6).

Commentators and writers have labored mightily to account for this apparent misplacement of the altar of incense. Some have rightly pointed out that, although the altar was in the Holy Place, its work connected closely with the Most Holy Place. The curtain separating the two apartments did not reach to the roof of the sanctuary, so that, when the priests offered incense on the golden altar, the cloud of fragrant intercession passed over and filled the Most Holy Place. Only with this protection did the high priest dare to enter the Most Holy Place every year during Israel's most solemn festival—the Day of Atonement (Lev. 6:12, 13). Further, on this high day, the high priest put the atoning blood on the horns of the golden altar—which is called "the altar that is before the Lord"—as well as on the mercy seat (NIV: atonement cover), in the Most Holy Place (vss. 14, 15).

Granted the validity of these observations, Paul's placement of the golden altar in the Most Holy Place remains a puzzle. His description of the sanctuary in Hebrews 9:1-5 merely lists the two apartments and their furnishings. He makes no attempt to explain here or later in the sermon the function of the golden altar or, for that matter, of any other item. Thus, all attempts to reason from the role of the golden altar in Leviticus 16 miss the mark.

I know of no satisfactory explanation for the apparent "mistake" in Hebrews 9:4. Rather than straining to find an answer, I think it best to simply acknowledge that the apostle made a slip here—a slip that makes no difference whatsoever to the argument of Hebrews. Of course, people who want to have every word of the Bible given directly by God will have a problem with this position, but they must deal with other places where the humanity of the Word, with its less-than-perfect transmission of ideas, is evident.

Ellen White's comments about so-called mistakes in the Bible give a helpful perspective.

> There is not always perfect order or apparent unity in the Scriptures. The miracles of Christ are not given in exact order, but are given just as the circumstances occurred, which called for this divine revealing of the power of Christ. The truths of the Bible are as pearls hidden. They must be searched, dug out by painstaking effort. Those who take only a surface view of the Scriptures will, with their superficial knowledge, which they think is very deep, talk of the contradictions of the Bible, and question the authority of the Scriptures. But those whose hearts are in harmony with truth and duty will search the Scriptures with a heart prepared to receive divine impressions. The illuminated soul sees a spiritual unity, one grand golden thread running through the whole, but it requires patience, thought, and prayer to trace out the precious golden thread. . . .
>
> The Bible is not given to us in grand superhuman language. Jesus, in order to reach man where he is, took humanity. The Bible must be given in the language of men. Everything that is human is imperfect. Different meanings are expressed by the same word; there is not one word for each distinct idea. The Bible was given for practical purposes (*Selected Messages*, 1:20).

More important than the "mistake" of Hebrews 9:3, 4 is the point the apostle wants to make in his description of the Mosaic sanctuary and its rituals. He indicates two fundamental inadequacies—limited access and limited cleansing.

Into the Holy Place, he tells us, entered the priests as they carried on their regular ministry. But only the high priest could enter the Most Holy Place, and that only once a year—on the Day of Atonement (vss. 6, 7). So only one person, and that only once every year, could enter into the very presence of God. The common person could not reach even to the outer apartment of the sanctuary.

Further, the various sacrifices and rituals in the sanctuary provided only ceremonial purification. They could not, says Paul, "clear the conscience of the worshiper" (vs. 9). They were an illustration pointing forward to the time when God would provide a decisive offering for sin.

As the discussion of Jesus' saving work develops in Hebrews 9:11–10:18, we shall see how these two points—access and cleansing—feature prominently in the apostle's thought. Chapter 9:1-10 lays the groundwork for the subsequent argument. And it is important to state again the relation between the old and the new that we noticed at the outset of this book. The old was not bad and the new good. Rather, the old was good, but the new is better, because with it comes finality. Unless we maintain this balance, we shall denigrate the old or collapse the new into the old—in either case missing the point of the argument of Hebrews.

A Hard Nut

With Hebrews 9:8, 9, we encounter one of the "hard nuts" of Scripture. It is worth our while to spend a few moments with it, because the attempt to crack it open exposes the issues of interpretation throughout the key chapters 9 and 10.

Fortunately, the apostle's overall meaning is clear. After sketching the Mosaic sanctuary and ritual in 9:1-7, he tells us that the Holy Spirit was showing by all this that a better way was yet to come, a way of which the old was an illustration (the Greek for "illustration" in verse 9 is *parabolē*—parable). Thus, he makes the point of limited access under the old system with the hint of a new day coming.

But how does he make this point? The answer depends on how we understand those Greek terms we noticed earlier—*ta hagia* (literally, "holy things" or "holy places") and *skēnē* ("tent").

Some commentators, such as Moffatt (117) and Westcott (252), argue that "the first tabernacle" of verse 8 must be understood from verse 6, since the wording is identical. (The New International Version confuses the reader by translating *skēnē* as "the outer room" in verse 6 but as "the first tabernacle" in verse 8.) That is, "the first tabernacle" is the Holy Place. They then understand *ta hagia* in verse 8 as the Most Holy Place and reach an interesting conclusion: The entire earthly sanctuary corresponds with the heavenly temple as the Holy Place to Most Holy. Thus, they contend, the outer apartment, the Holy, illustrated the entire earthly sanctuary with its limitations described in verse 9, but the second apartment represented the entire heavenly temple.

The implications of this interpretation are heavy. Rather than the heavenly temple having both a Holy and a Most Holy Place, it *is* the true Most Holy Place itself.

But we may see Hebrews 9:8, 9 in a different way. In my judgment we should go back to the beginning of the apostle's discussion of the sanctuary, where he has previously mentioned the heavenly temple—that is, to 8:1-6. There, *ta hagia* is rightly translated as "sanctuary" in the New International Version, with *skēnē* as "tabernacle" standing as a parallel expression. The contrast in 9:8, 9, then, isn't between the two apartments of the earthly sanctuary, with the Holy illustrating the earthly sanctuary and the Most Holy the heavenly, but between the two sanctuaries themselves—the earthly and the heavenly.

If one reads straight through from Hebrews 8:1–9:10, this interpretation emerges as the clear meaning that ties the entire passage together. To see the apostle making spiritual applications of the two apartments, as the first interpretation suggests, seems too subtle and out of line with his treatment in this passage and elsewhere in Hebrews.

A paraphrase will help bring out the meaning of Hebrews 9:8, 9, as I understand it: "The Holy Spirit showed by the Mosaic sanctuary and ritual that the way into the heavenly sanctuary had not been opened so long as the first sanctuary continued functioning. That sanctuary was an illustration pointing to the true sanctuary with its offering that would provide decisive cleansing."

The New International Version comes close to this view. Its interpretation of *skēnē*, "the first tabernacle," indicates the entire Mosaic sanctuary. However, by translating *ta hagia* as "Most Holy Place" instead of "sanctuary," it muddies the waters.

With Hebrews 9:10, the discussion of the better covenant, while not yet fully complete, has reached its zenith. But the sustained argument of 8:1–10:18 now takes on a larger context as it focuses on Christ's sacrifice. That will be our study in the next chapter.

■ Applying the Word

Hebrews 8:1–9:10

1. What does the covenant idea tell me about God?
2. How can I know whether I enjoy a covenant relationship with Him? What has He promised me? What have I promised Him?
3. As I contemplate the glory of the heavenly sanctuary, where Jesus ministers for me, what difference does it make to my Christian life to have such a belief?
4. How can I know for a certainty the supreme blessing of the new covenant—that my sins have been forgiven?
5. What values do I find in the Old Testament sanctuary and its services? What ideas from it seem strange in these modern times?
6. Hebrews 8 and 9 tell me about reality—but the reality is in heaven rather than on earth. How can I make the heavenly sanctuary as real in my life as the things on this earth that I can see and hear and touch?

■ Researching the Word

1. Use a concordance to look up the occurrences of the word *covenant* in the Old and the New Testament. What pattern or patterns do you find? How many covenants are

there? How does the presentation of covenant in Hebrews add to the overall picture? If you were giving a Bible study on this subject, how would you explain the significance of the idea of covenant for the spiritual life of Christians today?

2. Read through the book of Revelation, looking for references and allusions to the heavenly sanctuary. You may want to make a list. Compare these references to Paul's comments about the heavenly sanctuary in Hebrews 8 through 10. What similarities do you find? What differences? What spiritual insights about the heavenly sanctuary does Revelation provide, and how do these contribute to a better understanding of Paul's comments in Hebrews?

■ Further Study of the Word

1. For a discussion of the heavenly sanctuary, see W. G. Johnsson, "The Heavenly Sanctuary—Figurative or Real," in *Issues in the Book of Hebrews*, 35-51.
2. For a discussion of *ta hagia*, see A. P. Salom, "*Ta Hagia* in the Epistle to the Hebrews," in *Issues in the Book of Hebrews*, 219-227.
3. For discussions of typology in Hebrews, see R. M. Davidson, "Typology in the Book of Hebrews;" also A. R. Treiyer, "Antithetical or Correspondence Typology?" both in *Issues in the Book of Hebrews*, 121-186, and 187-198, respectively.

CHAPTER SEVEN

The Better Blood

Hebrews 9:11–10:18

Just as the first two chapters of Hebrews set forth the person of Christ in a series of glorious affirmations, so 9:11–10:18 declare and explain the glorious work He has accomplished for our salvation. And just as the apostle argued for Jesus' exalted person in contrast to angels, so here he presents His saving work against the inferior system of animal sacrifices.

This portion of Hebrews brings to a climax and a close the long theological discussion that began in 7:1. Indeed, with the great ideas presented here, the theology proper of the sermon reaches its conclusion. All that comes after may be seen as the "so what" following from the "what." With 7:1-28 taking up Christ's high-priestly order, the presentation as to His work begins at 8:1. Thus, as we have already seen, 8:1–10:18 is a unit in itself, but one that we chose to divide in order to handle the material more easily.

The argument of 9:11–10:18, then, flows directly out of the discussion of 8:1–9:10 that we have just considered. Those verses set the stage by laying out the Old Testament quotations and sanctuary services, which pointed themselves to God's great Sacrifice for sin—Jesus, who took our terrible problem of sin upon Himself and provided for us an eternal solution.

Hebrews 9:11–10:18 presents an ongoing, unbroken line of thought. We behold the wonder of our redemption in Jesus Christ, the God-Man, who dies on our behalf, a perfect, complete, once-for-all sacrifice for sin. By His dying He brings cleansing, not merely external but of the inner

being; and He throws open the doors of the heavenly temple to everyone
who accepts His atoning blood, and thereby He spells finished to the en-
tire system of animal sacrifices.

∎ Getting Into the Word

Hebrews 9:11–10:18

This portion of Hebrews is one of the most closely reasoned passages in all of Scripture. It will richly repay your
careful, concentrated study! When you grasp its magnificent
ideas, your heart will marvel at what God in Christ has done
for you, and you will rejoice in the assurance that His spilt
blood brings. Read Hebrews 9:11–10:18 twice in the New
International Version. Then read 8:1–10:18 at one sitting.
Seek answers to the following questions:

1. Look up all the references to blood in 8:1–10:18. Look
   up the other references to blood in Hebrews. Make a
   list, citing each reference and noting what blood does in
   each case. Find out whether blood is a positive or a negative agent.
2. As you study, remember that the New International Version consistently translates *ta hagia* as Most Holy Place
   in 9:11–10:18, whereas a more neutral translation would
   be "sanctuary." Study each place the New International
   Version mentions Most Holy Place, and decide from the
   context what you think the translation should be.
3. Look for and list any allusions to the Day of Atonement
   in Hebrews 8:1–10:18.
4. List expressions that point to Christ's sacrifice as the
   decisive answer to the sin problem.
5. List expressions that show how His sacrifice provides
   access to God's presence for us.
6. List expressions indicating that Calvary provided a single,
   nonrepeatable, complete sacrifice for sins.

7. Diagram Hebrews 10:11-14 by making two lists to contrast the work of the Old Testament priests and the work of Christ. The beginning of these lists is:

Earthly priests	*Christ's work*
Every priest (many)	This priest (one)
Day after day (repeated)	One sacrifice
_____	_____
_____	_____

9. Study the references to perfection in 10: 1, 14. Compare these with 7:11, 19. Note also 9:9, where the Greek reads "*perfect* the conscience." What conclusions do you draw with regard to the perfecting of Christians?

10. What does the "blood" of Christ mean in 9:11–10:18? Does it mean actual blood? If not, then what does it mean?

11. Hebrews 9:11–10:18 is perhaps the most detailed, comprehensive, systematic passage dealing with Christ's saving work in all of Scripture. From your study of it, try to state simply and clearly how God saves us through Jesus Christ. Does the passage answer all your questions about the plan of salvation? What questions can you think of that it does not answer?

■ Exploring the Word

Since 9:11–10:18 forms a tightly woven whole, we grasp it best by concentrating on its leading themes rather than attempting to break it into paragraphs for consecutive study. We shall therefore take up its presentation of the sin problem (defilement), the role of blood, the contrasts of the old and the new, the note of finality, and perfection. Finally, we shall discuss concerns from the passage that impact Seventh-day Adventist theology and our teaching of the heavenly sanctuary.

The Human Dilemma—Defilement

In Hebrews 1:3 the apostle summed up the earthly work of the Son with the words "He . . . provided purification for sins." Now, as he spells out that work, he again stresses its cleansing aspect.

- 9:13—Animal blood brings ceremonial purification to those who are outwardly unclean.
- 9:14—Christ's blood, however, cleanses the conscience.
- 9:22—Under the Old Testament system, almost everything was cleansed with blood.
- 9:23—The earthly things, which were copies of the heavenly, were purified with animal sacrifices, but the heavenly things required something better.
- 10:2—If animal sacrifices could have provided thorough cleansing, they would not have needed to be offered every year.

To these verses that enter into the deep theological reasoning of 9:11–10:18, we should add this reference from the exhortation that follows immediately: "having our hearts sprinkled to cleanse us from a guilty conscience and having our bodies washed with pure water" (10:22).

We see, then, that in the book of Hebrews, the human problem—the dilemma into which sin has placed us—is that we are defiled. We cannot come into the presence of a holy God, because we are unclean. Just as outward or ceremonial impurity barred the Israelites anciently from worshiping at the sanctuary, our impurity, which embraces the total being, keeps us from the heavenly reality.

Although occasionally in Hebrews we find other terms (such as *ransom*) used to describe Christ's saving work (9:15), the primary description is purification, as 1:3 indicated from the outset. Nor is 9:22 an exception: "Without the shedding of blood there is no forgiveness." The word translated "forgiveness," the Greek *aphesis*, has the idea of release or removal. In this verse the apostle uses it in parallel with "cleans[ing]," so its meaning must be similar.

This statement of the human dilemma surprises many Christians when they first encounter it. Protestants tend to be more familiar with the great books of the Reformation—Romans and Galatians. In these letters Paul's presentation of the plan of salvation centers in a different term—*justification*. Justification suggests a court model, where we stand accused of law breaking, but where One stands for us, and we are acquitted.

In fact, Scripture gives us a series of models or metaphors of Christ's work. Each model has its setting in daily, ordinary life. Take forgiveness, for instance. Here the problem is a debt that we find impossible to pay, but Christ's work cancels our debt, and we are forgiven. That is why we pray "Forgive us our debts" in the Lord's Prayer.

Reconciliation provides a quite different model. This one is drawn from the area of human relations, with sin being the implacable enmity separating us from God. Here, Christ's work removes the estrangement, and we are reconciled with our Maker. Other models include ransom (payment of a price), redemption (buying back), liberation, adoption, sanctification (another sanctuary term, signifying consecration or separation for God's use), and lost/found. In each case, sin is conceived of in a different manner, and in each case it presents humanity with a terrible dilemma, from which we cannot escape. But through Jesus Christ, we find a way out—He, in Himself, by His death, provides a full solution.

Students of the religions of humanity have observed the universal sense of defilement with which the sons and daughters of our first parents still struggle. Societies for whom the model of the law court may be foreign nevertheless have this sense of impurity before the Holy One. The French scholar Paul Ricoeur has traced the language of confession among the peoples of the world. He finds that the most basic confession, reducible to no other, is: I am dirty; I need cleansing from God.

Thus the book of Hebrews focuses on the human problem in a way that rings with universality. Its language of defilement and purification echoes the Old Testament book of Leviticus, with which it has so much in common and to which it provides the New Testament counterpart. But it reaches far beyond—to every person everywhere.

This language resonates with people in our day also—with us. We who believe sing with James Nicholson, "Now wash me, and I shall be whiter than snow." Or we sing with William Cowper:

> There is a fountain filled with blood,
> Drawn from Immanuel's veins;
> And sinners plunged beneath that flood,
> Lose all their guilty stains.

Hymns such as these touch chords deep within us. They express the reality of our sin problem and of Christ's work to set us free.

Nor is the language of defilement and cleansing restricted to Christians. We still find echoes and resonances in the expressions of secular society: "dirty money," "filthy story," "coming clean," and "dirty politics." Counselors often meet people who have an overwhelming sense of dirtiness. And then there is our passion for cleanliness, especially in America, with its huge bathrooms and massive water consumption—not to mention our sense of outrage at the pollution of our air and water.

The book of Hebrews speaks to our day with startling application!

Better Blood

Just as the apostle sets out the human dilemma in terms of defilement, so he presents the cleansing agent par excellence—blood. But not just any blood, and certainly not animal blood, which provides outward or ceremonial purification but cannot cleanse the conscience. No, Hebrews tells of better blood than all others—Christ's blood.

We see how the apostle's argument turns on blood at key points in this passage and beyond:

- 9:7—The Old Testament high priest never entered the Most Holy Place without blood.
- 9:12—Christ entered the heavenly sanctuary, not with the blood of goats and calves, but with His own blood.
- 9:13, 14—Animal blood provides ceremonial cleansing, but Christ's blood provides purification of conscience.
- 9:18-21—The first covenant was ratified with blood.
- 9:22—Under the old system, almost everything was cleansed with blood.
- 9:22—There is no putting away of sins without blood.
- 9:25—Christ did not enter the heavenly sanctuary with the blood of another.
- 10:4—It is impossible for the blood of animals to take away sins.
- 10:19—We have confidence to enter the heavenly sanctuary through Jesus' blood.
- 10:29—The person who despises the blood of the new covenant deserves severe punishment.
- 11:28—Moses kept the Passover and the sprinkling of blood.
- 12:24—Jesus' sprinkled blood "speaks a better word."

As we look at these references, we see that throughout the argument, blood is a superbly positive agent—one charged with divine power. Blood cleanses; blood provides access; blood ratifies the covenant; blood speaks God's good word to us.

We notice also that blood occupies the central place in the argument concerning the work of Christ. Although Paul at times employs the language of "sacrifice" (e.g., 9:23, 26; 10:1, 3, 8, 10, 12) and even "body" (10:5, 10), he reverts to "blood" for his decisive affirmations. Three great statements explain how God through Jesus Christ provides the solution to our terrible dilemma caused by sin.

- 9:13, 14—"The blood of goats and bulls and the ashes of a heifer sprinkled on those who are ceremonially unclean sanctify them so that they are outwardly clean. How much more, then, will the blood of Christ, who through the eternal Spirit offered himself unblemished to God, cleanse our consciences from acts that lead to death, so that we may serve the living God!"

- 9:22—"Without the shedding of blood there is no forgiveness."
  10:4—"It is impossible for the blood of bulls and goats to take away sins."

These affirmations stand like spiritual axioms. They open a window on the mind of God, providing us with a glimpse of His plan of atonement. Logically, these statements hang together as follows:

Basic axiom:
  Only through blood can sin be put away (9:22).
Related axioms:
  1. Animal blood can only provide cleansing of a ceremonial, external nature; it cannot ultimately deal with the sin problem (9:13; 10:4).
  2. Christ's blood, however, provides finality, the removal of sin once and for all (9:14).

With these ideas we look into the heart of God. We see, and yet we do not see. No other way—this is what we see. No other way out of our mess. No other way to get clean. No other way than the blood of Christ.

And yet we do not see. We do not see *why* there could be no other way, *why* without shedding of blood there could be no putting away of sin.

But God has shown us all He chooses to show. He has made plain *how* we can be saved, meaning that He has provided the way for us. He hasn't told us why He chose this way. He simply tells us that *this* is the way. He tells us that He has taken our terrible problem upon Himself, and He Himself has provided the answer.

That is all we need to know. By believing, by accepting His

provision, we find what we most need. The blood of Jesus Christ, His Son, cleanses us from all defilement.

A final thought about the better blood. The term *blood* seems reducible to no other. It signifies Christ's death—but more, His death applied to our problem of defilement. It points to Christ's life poured out for us—but more, life that gives us life, that brings cleansing and healing. Just as the language of defilement and purification strikes a deep response within our consciences, so the language of better blood speaks directly to our religious need in a manner that cannot be replaced by other terminology.

Those Christians—including some Adventists—who find Hebrews' concentration on blood for its key argumentation offensive need to look deeper. The presentation here is light years away from any concept of a pagan, bloodthirsty deity. It is full of grace and truth. And it speaks with clarity and force to each of us in these times.

Benefits of Christ's Blood

Throughout Hebrews 9:11–10:18, the accomplishment of Christ's sacrifice appears in contrast to the old system. All that the old failed to do—indeed, could not do—Jesus' better blood has done.

The two weaknesses of the old, we saw earlier, were its limited access and its limited cleansing. Hebrews 9:1-10 sketched the old cultus in a manner that highlighted these two deficiencies. But now in 9:11–10:18 Paul shows how the new system in Jesus removes these deficiencies.

Christ's blood, he immediately tells us, enabled Him to enter the heavenly sanctuary—"The greater and more perfect tabernacle that is not man-made, that is to say, not a part of this creation" (9:11). He comes back to the thought in 9:24: "Christ did not enter a man-made sanctuary that was only a copy of the true one; he entered heaven itself, now to appear for us in God's presence."

We see the radical contrast the author draws with the Mosaic

sanctuary. There, only one person on one day out of the year attained to the presence of God. And, in fact, the high priest's entering into the Most Holy Place on Yom Kippur each year was
even more restricted in its approach to reality, because the sanctuary in which he ministered was but a shadow of the ultimately
real.

Unhindered access to the divine presence—this is the point of
9:11, 12, 24. And this access isn't just for Jesus, who offered His
better blood—it is for us also. Summing up his long discussion
that started at 8:1, the apostle in 10:19 declares, "*We* have confidence to enter the [heavenly sanctuary] by the blood of Jesus."

These verses echo and complement the affirmation of 4:16: "Let
us then approach the throne of grace with confidence, so that we
may receive mercy and find grace to help us in our time of need."
Indeed, the word translated "approach" in 4:16 is the same as that
translated "draw near" in 10:22. The Greek *proserchomai* signifies
the high priest's entry into the very presence of God.

The apostle is telling us that *we* Christians are now like the
earthly high priests who, alone, could come into the Most Holy
Place. But whereas they had that privilege on but one day every
year, we have it every day of the year. And while they entered a
Most Holy Place that was only a copy of the true, we come to the
heavenly reality.

We do not come with fear and cringing. We come not with hat
in hand. *We come confidently.* Our holy boldness rests, not in ourselves, but in two facts about Jesus Christ. First, He understands
us. He, our great High Priest, has walked in our shoes, understands our trials and pain, and knows just what we need most.
Second, His blood has broken down the old barriers that separated humanity from God. His blood provides full, complete
cleansing from sin; His blood opens the doors of the heavenly
temple—to us!

Of course, we do not physically enter the heavenly sanctuary
now. We enter by faith, and faith makes us sure of what we do not
see (11:1). We do not walk by sight, for we look to ultimate realities. And Jesus, the Son of God, who became one with us, has

guaranteed them for us. That is why we "draw near to God with a sincere heart in full assurance of faith" (10:22).

For His blood provides thorough cleansing from sin—that is its second superlative benefit. We see this thought reiterated throughout 9:11–10:18:

- 9:14—Christ's blood provides not merely ceremonial purification (9:13) but total cleansing.
- 9:15—Christ's death sets people free from sins committed under the first covenant (that is, under the Mosaic sanctuary).
- 9:23—The heavenly sanctuary requires better sacrifices than the blood of animals.
- 9:25, 26—Christ entered heaven, not with other blood, but by virtue of His own sacrifice. And this sacrifice does away with sin.
- 9:28—Christ was sacrificed once to take away sins.
- 10:10—Christ's sacrifice has made us holy.
- 10:14—Christ's sacrifice has perfected us forever.
- 10:18—Christ's sacrifice brings all other sacrifices to an end, because they are no longer needed.

And the upshot for daily Christian living? We approach God in His heavenly temple with holy boldness, "having our hearts sprinkled to cleanse us from a guilty conscience and having our bodies washed with pure water" (10:22).

The book of Hebrews rings with Christian confidence. Its affirmations about access and cleansing from sin are unmatched in force and beauty. And the reason is simple: This book, inspired by the Holy Spirit, devotes so much attention to both the person and the saving work of our Lord.

In wrapping up this discussion of the benefits of Christ's blood, we should notice briefly 9:16, 17. Translations of these verses vary widely, and, while our overall understanding of 9:11–10:18 is not affected by these differences, we should understand what lies behind them.

The issue in translation involves the Greek word *diathēkē*, which we encountered earlier. This word can mean either "covenant" or "will," and while the New International Version translators render it as "covenant" everywhere else in Hebrews, in 9:16, 17, they translate it as "will." Since in 15, 18 the word has to mean "covenant"—and they so translate it—they have the author playing on the word's twofold meaning in 16, 17. Many commentators agree with this line of thought, being influenced by the linking of *diathēkē* and death in these two verses.

I think this line of reasoning is flawed. It is too subtle and breaks the development of the covenant idea that began in chapter 8 and reaches its denouement in 10:18. The apostle is talking about *covenant* throughout—not switching to "will" for two verses and immediately dropping back to covenant. And the linking of covenant with death is precisely his point: The *death* of Christ alone establishes the new covenant. Verse 15 made that assertion: "Christ is the mediator of a new covenant . . . now that he has died."

Finality—Once for All

Hebrews' contrast between the old and the new comes into sharp focus in a particular term—*once* or *once for all*. We first find this idea in 7:27, where we learn that Christ offered himself once for all. In 9:11–10:18, however, it becomes a leading thought:

- 9:12—Christ entered the heavenly sanctuary once for all by His blood.
- 9:26—He came once for all to do away with sins.
- 9:28—He was sacrificed once to take away sins.
- 10:10—We have been made holy by Christ's sacrifice once for all. Hebrews portrays Christ's once-for-all ministry in the heavenly tabernacle in vivid contrast to the ongoing ministry of the priests in the earthly tabernacle.
- 9:6—The priests carry on regular, that is, repeated, ministry.
- 9:25—The earthly sanctuary required repeated offerings.
- 10:1—The same sacrifices were repeated endlessly year after year.

- 10:3—Annual sacrifices were offered on the Day of Atonement.
- 10:11—The priests offered the same sacrifices again and again.

With these statements, we see the third of the apostle's contrasts in 9:11–10:18—not only full access to the heavenly temple instead of limited access to its copy and not only thorough cleansing from sin instead of merely ceremonial purification, but also one sacrifice instead of many. One sacrifice for all time, never to be repeated. One sacrifice for all peoples. Once. Once for all. A sacrifice that does the job. A sacrifice that brings all other sacrifices to a halt, because they aren't needed anymore.

Hebrews' note of "once for all" stresses *what has already happened.* In theological parlance, this is called "realized eschatology"—what Christ has already accomplished. Yes, the apostle recognizes that there is more to come, that the plan of salvation is yet to reach its finale. (Hebrews 9:27, 28 points to the second coming, when Jesus will come back, "not to bear sin.") But his emphasis falls on what already *is.* That is why the New International Version correctly translates 9:11, "When Christ came as high priest of the good things *that are already here*," as compared to the King James Version's, "But Christ being come an high priest of good things *to come.*"

We can see the comparisons and contrasts of the old and new in 9:23-26 and again in 10:11-14. Note how in 9:23-26 the apostle highlights the superior nature and benefits of the blood of Christ:

Old System	New System
Purified	Purified
By blood	By blood
But	
Only copies of the reality	The true sanctuary
Blood "not his own"	Sacrifice of Himself
Repeated sacrifices	Once for all
Earthly—Most Holy	Heavenly—Presence of God

Hebrews 10:11-14 brings these contrasts into even sharper focus. In this paragraph he pulls together the various strands of reasoning that have run from 8:1 onward, and following this he concludes with a citation from the Old Testament as the final clincher of his argument. The apostle summarizes the benefits of Christ's sacrifice in contrast to the entire old system:

Old System	New System
Every priest (i.e., many)	Christ (only one)
stands (unfinished work)	sat down (completed)
offers (ongoing work)	offered (finished)
same sacrifices	one sacrifice
again and again	for all time
day after day	offering complete
his religious duties (limited access)	right hand of God
never take away sins	made perfect forever

As we reflect on the masterful presentation of Hebrews 9:1–10:18, two observations come to mind. First, we see how precious Jesus' blood is, and how great are its benefits! Throughout human history, men and women have felt alienated from Deity, cut off, inadequate to come before Him. They have sought to gain access through priests and shamans, through pilgrimages, penance, and pain, through ablutions and self-mortification. But the glorious message of Hebrews is that now, already, a way to God has opened! Through Jesus Christ, *in* Jesus Christ, we have full, unlimited access and full, unlimited cleansing from our terrible defilement.

Second, the old system, which appears so inadequate in this presentation, was nevertheless from God. He set it up. It was the way of righteousness by faith in its own time. The person who trusted Yahweh did what He instructed, which was to offer an animal sacrifice for sins. The benefits of that system—its teaching about the seriousness of sin and the role of blood, its pointing forward to Christ, and so on—are not taken up here. But they were real. To dismiss the Old Testament sanctuary service out of hand because of its seeming strangeness to our modern sensibilities denigrates the Old Testament and its God—who is the God of the book of Hebrews.

What—Perfect Already?

In Hebrews 10:14, concluding his discussion of the benefits of Christ's sacrifice, Paul makes a startling statement: "By one sacrifice he has made perfect forever those who are being made holy." Here we seem to have instantaneous, permanent perfection that cannot be lost!

However, a study of his other declarations in Hebrews concerning the perfecting of believers reveals a consistent pattern—one that exposes how wrongheaded are many of the discussions about perfection in which Christians engage today. We find the first references in chapter 7, where we learn that perfection could not be attained through the Levitical priesthood (vs. 11) and that "the law [of the priesthood under the old system] made nothing perfect" (vs. 19).

Hebrews 9:11–10:18 has three other references to perfection. The first one doesn't appear in the New International Version, but the Greek text of 9:9 reads literally "make *perfect* the conscience" instead of "clear the conscience." This text stands in obvious parallel with 9:14, where we read that, in contrast to the blood of goats and bulls, Christ's blood can "*cleanse* our consciences." That is, in 9:9, 14 perfection and conscience are tied together, with perfection being equivalent to cleansing.

The next reference to perfection occurs in 10:1, where the author tells us that the repeated sacrifices of the old system could not "make perfect those who draw near to worship." The following two verses are enlightening. Verse 2 tells us that if animal sacrifices could have done the job, "the worshipers would have been cleansed once for all," and verse 3 states that the repeated sacrifices "are an annual reminder of sins." We find here precisely the same conclusion as in 9:9, 14—that "perfection" signifies "cleansing."

In fact, the parallel with 9:9, 14 goes even farther. Although the New International Version has failed to translate it, the same word for conscience as in 9:9, 14—the Greek *suneidēsis*—occurs in 10:2. Where the New International Version translates, "Would no longer have felt guilty for their sins," the original reads literally, "Would no longer have a conscience of sins." In my judgment, those who worked on the New International Version have captured the apostle's thought accurately here and also in 9:9, where they used *clear* instead of *perfect*, but their decision to translate the same Greek words (for perfection and conscience) in different ways hampers the careful student of Hebrews who wishes to come to grips with the apostle's terminology.

We now see what Paul means by perfection in this book. His five references link the idea to the sanctuary—his first two (7:11, 19) to the old system in general and his last three specifically to sacrifice (9:9; 10:2, 14). Under the old system, he reasons, there was no perfection, because animal sacrifices simply could not purify the inner being. If they could have, they would not have had to be repeated year after year. But Christ has come and offered Himself, and that sacrifice does what all the blood under the old system could never do—it has brought cleansing of the conscience. By this one sacrifice, then, "he has made perfect forever those who are being made holy" (10:14).

These ideas are light-years away from the context in which some Christians think of perfection. Perfection here has nothing to do with victorious living or the successive elimination of sins from the life. Valid as that idea is, it is not the apostle's point in this passage. Perfection here is something *already* achieved, something *already* fixed and certain. Furthermore, it has nothing to do with what *we* labor to achieve, because it has come by what *Christ* has already done *for* us.

In our study earlier in the book about the person of Jesus, we noticed how the language of perfection was used of His human experiences. For Him, perfection did not signify sinful habits to be overcome, but rather maturation into the office of High Priest. And the discussion about the perfection of His followers in Hebrews 9, 10 further demonstrates how misconceived are many current debates on this topic.

To many sincere believers struggling in the battle with sin, the teaching of Hebrews will come as a surprise and a shock. When we let it sink into our souls, however, it will come as a liberating word—a word of hope and assurance. It will point us away from ourselves and to Jesus; it will point us back, instead of forward, to what He has already done for us by His death for us rather than what we must do.

Getting right with God and feeling right with God—this is the quest that has occupied men and women throughout history. In a passage that crowns the thought of the Old Testament, the prophet Micah framed the age-old question: "With what shall I come before the Lord and bow down before the exalted God?" Then, in an escalating series, he suggests the ways by which humankind has attempted to find an answer: "Shall I come before him with burnt offerings, with calves a year old? Will the Lord be pleased with thousands of rams, with ten thousand rivers of oil? Shall I offer my firstborn for my transgression, the fruit of my body for the sin of my soul?" (Micah 6:6, 7).

And to every option he presents, our hearts cry out: No! No! No! No sacrifice of a calf or a lamb can make us worthy to stand in Yahweh's presence, not a thousand or ten thousand, and certainly not the offering of our child as a human sacrifice! For sin is a moral problem. If, in a fit of rage, I rise up and kill another person, what can I do to make matters right? I may slay a lamb—but how can that help? Now on the ground lies a dead lamb alongside the dead man! A thousand or ten thousand or a million sacrifices cannot remove my guilt.

That is what Hebrews is telling us in its reasoning about perfection and conscience. All the provisions of the old system, all the sacrifices repeated year after year, could never bring finality to the sin problem. Indeed, their very repetition proclaimed that the problem was still there, that the people's consciences—or consciousness of sin—had not been set at rest.

God alone could provide the answer. And He did. By sending

His Son to become one with us and to die on our behalf, He did what untold billions of sacrifices could not accomplish. God took our problem, our dilemma, upon Himself. His self-sacrifice provides "better blood" indeed! His sacrifice makes us whole—*now*! Gone is the weary round of sacrifices—endless, repeated, taking humankind nowhere. Gone forever, because by that one Sacrifice, sin has been cleansed forever, and ultimately it will be banished forever.

Searching Questions

We turn now to areas of special concern to Seventh-day Adventists. Because of our interest in the heavenly sanctuary, where Jesus ministers as our great High Priest, Hebrews has attracted our close attention from the days of our pioneers. This book stands as the counterpart of Leviticus, interpreting, explaining, and applying the Old Testament rituals.

Of particular interest is the Day of Atonement. Seventh-day Adventists believe and teach that the antitype of Yom Kippur— the highest holy day in the Jewish calendar—commenced in 1844, when Jesus began His second-apartment ministry in a work of judgment that immediately precedes His return to earth.

These distinctive doctrines have come under attack throughout the course of Seventh-day Adventist history, with some of the sharpest thrusts coming from Adventists or former Adventists themselves. In recent years Dr. Desmond Ford has gathered together past critiques and sharpened them. And he argues strongly from Hebrews.

According to Ford, the Day of Atonement plays a vital role in the argument of Hebrews. The apostle, he says, describes Christ's work on Calvary as the antitype of Yom Kippur, so that on His ascension He entered the Most Holy Place in the heavenly sanctuary. If Ford is correct in his interpretation, the Adventist understanding of 1844 is obviously untrue to Scripture.

In my judgment, Dr. Ford misconstrues the place of the Day of Atonement in Hebrews. The Day of Atonement enters into the argument, but not to the extent or in the manner that Ford suggests. The Day of Atonement isn't *the* key Old Testament type against which the apostle frames his argument, but is merely *one* of *all* the rituals that comprised the old system. The argument doesn't proceed as Calvary/Day of Atonement, but rather Calvary/Mosaic sacrifices in toto. We find many references to sacrifices in Hebrews:

- 5:1-3—"Gifts and sacrifices for sins."
- 7:27—Daily sacrifices for sins.
- 9:9,10—"Gifts and sacrifices . . . food and drink . . . various ceremonial washings."
- 9:12—"The blood of goats and calves."
- 9:13—"The blood of goats and bulls and the ashes of a heifer."
- 9:18-21—Ratification of the first covenant by the blood of calves.
- 10:8—Sacrifices, offerings, burnt offerings, sin offerings.
- 10:11—Daily services of the old system.
- 10:29—"The blood of the covenant."
- 11:4—The sacrifice offered by Abel.
- 11:28—The blood of the Passover.
- 12:24—The blood of the new covenant.
- 13:11—Sacrifices of the high priest.

Thus, we see that the apostle argues from the full range of Old Testament rituals that involved blood. Among these was the Day of Atonement, and we find references to it in at least three places (9:7, 25; 10:1-3). The mention of the high priest and/or an *annual* ritual specifies these texts as indicating Yom Kippur. Here alone, I think, we should translate our old friend *ta hagia* as "Most Holy Place" rather than by the more neutral "sanctuary" (13:11 may provide a fourth allusion to the Day of Atonement, but the apostle's reasoning there seems to run in a different vein, as we shall see later).

The Day of Atonement, therefore, was but one among many rituals. It was the high point of Israel's sacrificial system, but even so—and this is the apostle's point—it could not provide access to God or deal decisively with sin. So far as sacrifices are concerned, Jesus' death on Calvary provided the antitype of them all—the Day of Atonement included. Jesus died in A.D. 31, not 1844. But the Day of Atonement in Israel's sanctuary involved more than the killing of animals. It centered in the removal of sin from the camp and making a fresh start for the entire people. Adventists see these aspects in God's Day of Atonement commencing in 1844, when the Lord Himself took in hand winding up the long controversy between good and evil.

Over the years, some Adventists have tried to find more in the book of Hebrews to support our distinctive teachings of the sanctuary and the judgment than the text permits. Their endeavors have been aided and abetted by the various translations, the King James Version and Revised Standard Version included, which have given inconsistent and even faulty translations of *ta hagia*. But Ford and others who have sought to discredit these doctrines on the basis of Hebrews have erred on the other side.

Hebrews provides the clearest statement of the heavenly sanctuary. It asserts unequivocally the existence of this temple and the ministry of Jesus in it as our great High Priest. Thereby, Hebrews provides the basis from which proceeds our unique understanding of our Lord's heavenly work.

And Hebrews goes farther. In 9:23 it states the *necessity* that the heavenly sanctuary be purified. This text has caused exegetes and commentators to stand on their heads in an endeavor to explain it—which has usually meant explaining it away. Some have tried to argue that "the heavenly things" that need cleansing are the same as the "conscience" in 9:9, 14 or that *purified* in 9:23 means "inaugurate." Both suggestions fail totally in light of the complete discussion that runs through 8:1–10:18, where the argument clearly revolves around defilement, purification, and Christ's heavenly work.

But to Seventh-day Adventists, with our heightened awareness of this terminology because of Daniel 8:14—"Unto two thousand and three hundred days, then shall the sanctuary be cleansed"

(KJV)—the statement of Hebrews 9:23 does not present a problem at all. We understand heaven and earth to be interconnected, so that events on earth have cosmic ramifications and touch heaven itself. God's working out the sin problem, we understand, extends to the very heart of the universe. And Christ's sacrifice—the better blood—provides the complete answer, cleansing all that needs to be cleansed, whether on earth or in heaven.

Hebrews 9:23 leaves open the time of the heavenly purification. From our study of Daniel and Revelation, we understand it to have begun in 1844.

One searches in vain for any elaboration of 9:23 in the rest of Hebrews. It is a passing comment, pregnant with meaning, enigmatic and troubling to many commentators and other Christians, but full of significance for Seventh-day Adventists. As we have noticed throughout 8:1–10:18, the apostle primarily looks backward. His gaze is fixed on Calvary, to that decisive moment in history that he calls "the end of the ages" (9:26). There, the God-Man offered up Himself. There, He provided an all-sufficient, atoning sacrifice that once-for-all gave the answer to the human dilemma. There, He won the decisive battle and guaranteed the outcome of the long struggle with evil.

Occasionally, Paul looks to the future. He tells us early on in Hebrews that the Son, who sits at the Father's right hand—the place of honor, signifying that His work has been successful—awaits the time when all the universe will come back to Him (1:12, 13). He speaks of the second coming, when Jesus "will appear a second time, not to bear sin, but to bring salvation to those who are waiting for him" (9:28). And he speaks also about future judgment (10:30, 31; 12:25-29). But he does not elaborate these themes. Throughout the book, his focus is more on the past—Calvary—than on the future.

So we come at last to the conclusion of the theological argument of Hebrews on the work of Christ that began at 8:1. Especially from 9:11–10:18, the reasoning has been close and intense—and it certainly isn't light reading! But what wonderful ideas emerge for the delight and nurture of the earnest seeker! What mind-boggling conceptions, what certainty, what assurance!

Yes, even now, we *belong*, says the apostle. Even now, we have access to the throne room of the universe. Even now, Jesus has cleansed us from guilt, lifted our heavy burden, and set us free. There is no need to look to any other temple, any other sacrifice, any deed, or any deity. We need look only to Jesus. His blood—oh, what better blood!—has made us whole, given us new status with the Father, opened the doors of heaven, and given us divine confidence.

With 10:18 the theology of Hebrews reaches it climax and conclusion. From the great WHAT, it has established the SO WHAT that follows, which will continue to the close of the sermon.

■ Applying the Word

Hebrews 9:11–10:18

1. To understand the teaching that Jesus is our great High Priest is to exchange fear for hope. To grasp His work as our all-sufficient sacrifice is to exchange doubt for full assurance. What passages in Hebrews 9:11–10:18 especially give me this hope and assurance?
2. What would the blood of a sacrificial lamb have meant to a person in Old Testament times? What does Christ's "better blood" (9:11-14) mean to me today? Because of this difference, in what ways can my walk with God be better than someone who lived before Christ?
3. What does it mean to me to have access to the heavenly temple? What, if anything, can I do to gain entrance into God's presence right now?
4. How can the lessons in Hebrews 9:11–10:18 help me to feel worthy, accepted, and welcome when I approach God in prayer?
5. Is my conscience cleansed from guilt and uncertainty? If it is not, how can this part of Hebrews help me gain that experience?

6. How has my understanding of sin and the wonder of God's saving provision increased during my study of this part of Hebrews?
7. What hymn or gospel song comes to mind as I contemplate the great ideas of this passage?
8. How does Christ's sacrifice make me "perfect forever" (10:14)? In what sense can I with confidence claim to be perfect? How can I be perfect at the same time that God is making me holy?

■ Researching the Word

1. Study the Day of Atonement in Leviticus 16. Then read through the book of Hebrews and list all the references to it. What does Leviticus say about the meaning and purpose of the day, and what does Hebrews say that goes beyond the explanation found in Leviticus?
2. With the aid of a concordance, look up all the references in the New Testament outside the book of Hebrews to *perfect* and *perfection*. Make a list of those texts where the emphasis is Christian perfection. Make a separate list of the references to perfection in Hebrews. What do the texts elsewhere in the New Testament add to your understanding of what Hebrews says about perfection, and how does Hebrews contribute to what other parts of the New Testament say?

■ Further Study of the Word

1. For further study concerning the Day of Atonement in Hebrews, see W. G. Johnsson, "Day of Atonement Allusions," in *Issues in the Book of Hebrews*, 105-120.
2. For discussion concerning Hebrews 9:23, see W. G. Johnsson, "Defilement/Purification and Hebrews 9:23," in *Issues in the Book of Hebrews*, 79-104.
3. For consideration of key passages, see H. Kiesler, "An Ex-

egesis of Selected Passages," in *Issues in the Book of Hebrews*, 53-78.

4. For theological considerations, especially regarding the sanctuary, see A. P. Salom, "Sanctuary Theology," in *Issues in the Book of Hebrews*, 199-218.

PART FOUR

Living in View of Jesus' Achievement

Hebrews 10:19–13:25

CHAPTER EIGHT

The Better Country

Hebrews 10:19–11:40

One year, when members of the Seventh-day Adventist Church studied the book of Hebrews, I heard the teacher of the day begin his introduction to chapter 11 with: "At last we have a lesson we can understand!" Some readers of this book may also feel a bit like that. The long theological section that began at 7:1 is heavy, especially in 9:11–10:18. But it comes loaded with rewarding insights and inspiring concepts to the diligent seeker.

All that follows applies the theology of this section and of the earlier chapters to Christian living. Just as we have encountered a series of practical passages, beginning with 2:1-4 and interspersed among the ongoing argumentation, so 10:19–13:25 will close out the work in a sustained exhortation of great power.

We can view the theology as the "WHAT" and the exhortations as the "SO WHAT." I believe the SO WHAT forms the chief purpose of the book. Hebrews is a "word of exhortation" (13:22), a sermon prepared to meet specific needs, and the theological sections provide the rational and inspirational framework.

In this long closing application, 10:19–13:25, we will meet again ideas already found in the earlier exhortations. Some merely reappear, but others are taken much farther, with one—faith (Greek: pistis)— emerging as the apostle's central concern.

While 10:19–13:25 comes as a continuous passage, we will divide it into two parts for convenience of study. The first, 10:19–11:40, focuses on faith in the "better country" (11:16) as the goal of Christians. The final chapter of our book will take up the apostle's concluding concerns in 12:1–13:25, with the better city—the heavenly Jerusalem—coming to the fore.

■ Getting Into the Word

Hebrews 10:19-39

Read Hebrews 10:19-39 through twice, thoughtfully and prayerfully. Then ask yourself the following questions:

1. In 10:19-25, find three great facts that give believers assurance, and find three concerns for Christian living that follow from such assurance.
2. Hebrews 10:26-31 presents another of the difficult passages of Hebrews. How does our study of 6:4-6 earlier help you to understand this passage?
3. List all the information about the addressees—the original readers of Hebrews—that this portion of the book provides. From this information, do you conclude that they were "new" or "old" Christians?
4. Look up Hebrews 10:19, 20 in different translations, including the New English Bible. What major differences do you notice concerning the interpretation of the "flesh" or "body" of Christ.
5. What was the attitude of these early Christians to the second coming?

■ Exploring the Word

Hebrews in Miniature

In Hebrews 10 the exhortation swings from strong warning (vss. 26-31) to strong encouragement (vss. 32-39). But first comes a seven-verse cameo that sums up both the theological argument that has just concluded and the counsel that will follow. If one is looking for a single passage that encapsulates the entire book, this is it.

With three striking affirmations, Hebrews 10:19-25 pulls together the theology of the first ten chapters—the "what" of Christian faith. Then the apostle gathers up our response to these surpassing privileges and benefits in three strong applications—the "so what" of Christian living. To grasp these seven verses is to discern the thrust and basis of the entire sermon.

We have confidence to enter the heavenly sanctuary, we have a great high priest in heaven, and we have hearts cleansed from a guilty conscience—these ringing assertions focus all the theological argument that has structured the first ten chapters of Hebrews. They show us, on the one hand, how deeply rooted is the apostle's thought in the sanctuary, and on the other, how great is the salvation that Jesus has brought, surpassing all that came before.

The first and third assertions—access and cleansing—come directly from the long discussion of 8:1–10:18, while the second is *the* point, the pith, of the first seven chapters. We have seen how Jesus' person and work combine to bring about these achievements. Thus 10:19-22 echoes and enlarges the earlier affirmation of 4:14-16:

> "Therefore, since we have a great high priest . . . let us then approach the throne of grace with confidence."

> "Therefore, brothers, since we have confidence to enter the [heavenly sanctuary] by the blood of Jesus . . . and since we have a great priest over the house of God."

Both passages use the same Greek word, *parrēsia*, translated "confidence" in the New International Version but "boldness" in the King James Version.

While the order of blessings outlined in 10:19-22 does not follow the development of the book (which is high priest, access, cleansing), it is surely the right one. Throughout 8:1–10:18 the apostle has lifted the reader's view to the heavenly temple, and in summary he says, And *we* have entry to that temple. Further, its high priest is one who loves and accepts us—our Saviour, Lord, and Friend, Jesus, the God-Man. Nor need we feel unworthy to approach this holy site, because Jesus' blood has made us clean within and without.

It is as though we have found ourselves transported to heaven and have found the door open. Gingerly we walk inside, wondering what lies beyond. We look around and up and see the magnificence of the heavenly sanctuary, glorious in form, color, and song. Just as we are wondering if we belong there, Jesus comes up to us and greets us. He escorts us and introduces us to the heavenly community. We meet the unfallen beings from other worlds and feel unworthy, but He brushes our fears aside, saying: "You belong here. You are My friend."

The passage vibrates with certainty. Along with *parrēsia* (confidence, boldness), we hear *plērophoria*—conviction, full assurance (vs. 22). Here is the answer to the Christian's doubts and fears, his or her times when the spiritual fires burn low and doubt attacks faith; and also to the loss of nerve in the face of our continuing weakness and falling short of God's ideal plan for us. Even in the best of spiritual times, who can say that he or she has done enough for Jesus? Who can claim perfect trust? Who has fully overcome temptation or blessed others by word and deed, as did the Saviour?

Not in us but in Him. Not in who we are but in who He is. Not in what we have done but in what He has done. There lies our confidence, our assurance. *He* is our assurance.

Christian certainty, then, isn't an emotional high we get from pumping ourselves up and getting others to pump us up. Our assurance rests on facts, not feelings. Those facts are, first of all, a Person and, second, His accomplishment. Every human system may fail and will fail. Every human society and organization will pass away. At the end of it all, one Fact remains—Jesus. At the end of the world, at the end of our world, only Jesus.

How, then, shall we live? In view of these facts—in view of Jesus—what does the good news mean for daily living? Three things in particular, Paul suggests as he goes on from 10:19-22 to summarize his exhortations in Hebrews.

First, "Let us hold unswervingly to the hope we profess" (vs. 23). Christ died for all, but we have an individual work to do. Christ brought salvation to all, but salvation does not come automatically. We must accept it and hold it.

We live in an age of unbelief. Cynics have come to full influence. The media specializes in bad news, and we believe it readily. Good news we question, and miracles we reject out of hand. How can Christians hold on in this age of doubt? By exercising the will to believe. We cannot *prove* the truths of our religion—the great affirmations of Hebrews 10:19-22—because they aren't subject to scientific investigation. History will confirm that there was a man named Jesus whom the Romans crucified—that is all. *Who* this person was and *what* His living and dying meant to the world reach beyond history and into the realm of faith.

We can choose to believe, or we can choose the way of cynics. God by His Spirit awakens faith and makes our choice a possibility, but ultimately, *we* must exercise the will to believe. We believe once, the first time, when we accept Jesus and His gift of salvation. But we believe over and over again as we continue to accept Him by exercising the will to believe.

We do not want a feeble, doubting Christianity. "Let us hold *unswervingly*," says the apostle (vs. 23). In the midst of this age of doubt, let faith shine forth. While others grope and wander, roaming the world in search of answers, let us keep our eyes fixed on Jesus and live life to the full. Secure in His love, confident of His acceptance, bold in our access to the heavenly courts, let us go gladly forward.

Second, "Let us consider how we may spur one another on toward love and good deeds" (vs. 24). We are more than ourselves; we are part of a body, a fellowship of believers. Individually we hold on to Christ unswervingly, but from and for one another we seek a ministry of nurture and encouragement. As doubt and skepticism multiply by sharing, so does faith. By talking faith and sharing faith, by exercising the will to believe first for ourselves, we help others to choose the option of faith for themselves.

Considering how we may spur each other on in love and good deeds—what a marvelous concept! Not looking at our neighbor to point the finger or to envy, but to build him or her up, to promote and stir to a life that mirrors the Master's. What a loving study of one another here, what sensitivity, what appreciation of individuality, what valuing of every brother and sister!

Third, "Let us not give up meeting together" (vs. 25). The electronic church can never take the place of corporate worship. As we join hearts and voices, we affirm that Christ has made us one through His cross. We belong to each other, just as we belong to Him; we need each other, just as we need Him. We learn from each other; we grow together. Jesus is too big to be encompassed by any one life, but together—corporately—we reflect His image.

By getting up and going to church instead of lying abed or spending the day to ourselves, we exercise the will to believe. We demonstrate faith—to ourselves and to our brothers and sisters in Christ. Let others go their own way—that was a problem already among the Hebrews; we will go to meeting.

For the Day—His day—is approaching. It was near for the Hebrew Christians; how much closer it is for us. We don't know when He will come back, but we know that He will come. One day, when people least expect Him, Christians included, He will return. So, in these days of unbelief, let us gather warmth from the coldness of others; let us "press together, press together," holding fast to our hope, building each other up in Christ, and meeting together to worship Him and to encourage each other.

Three glorious facts. Three practical results. The "what" of the gospel calls for the "so what" of Christian living.

As the theology of the first ten chapters focuses on these three facts, so the exhortations that comprise the remainder of the book will merely enlarge these three "so whats." And, we shall see, the key idea to emerge in the apostle's development will be faith—the will to believe.

Before we leave Hebrews 10:19-25, we should note a disputed point of interpretation. The issue concerns the relationship between the curtain and Jesus' body (or flesh, the literal translation) in verses 19, 20. The New International Version, along with many other versions, equates curtain with body. That is, we are to understand Paul's language of the curtain as expressing a spiritual truth. Commentators who see the passage in this way understand the reasoning as follows:

> Nor is there any difficulty in supposing that our author could explain the veil as being our Lord's "flesh"; like "the body of Jesus Christ" in v. 10 and "the blood of Jesus" in v. 19, "his flesh" here could mean His human life, offered up in sacrifice to God. It is by His sacrifice that the way of approach to God has been opened up. The veil which, from one point of view, kept God and mankind apart, can be thought of, from another point of view, as bringing them together; for it was one and the same veil which on one side was in contact with the glory of God and on the other side with the need of men and women. So in our Lord Godhead and manhood were brought together; he is the true "daysman" or umpire who can lay his hand upon both because He shares the nature of both. And by His death, it could be added, the "veil" of his flesh was rent asunder and the new way consecrated through it by which human beings may come to God (Bruce, *Epistle to the Hebrews*, 252).

I think this interpretation is incorrect. Throughout 8:1–10:18, we have seen no reason to take the apostle's sanctuary language in any way other than literally. He sets forth a *real* heavenly sanctuary with a *real* high priest and a *real* offering. To suddenly introduce a spiritualizing note here, so that the curtain (veil) in the heavenly sanctuary is a code word for Christ's body, jars with all that has gone before.

The Greek text can be understood in a different manner, so that the new way opened by Jesus is the way of His flesh—that is, provided by the Incarnation. One finds this interpretation in the New English Bible, which I think has rightly captured the intent of the passage: "So now, my friends, the blood of Jesus makes us free to enter boldly into the sanctuary by the new, living way which he has opened for us through the curtain, the way of his flesh."

Solemn Warning

In an abrupt change of mood, the apostle turns from ringing assurance to earnest appeal. He tells us (vss. 16-31) that entrance to the eternal future God has prepared for us doesn't follow automatically. Just as summary judgment fell on those people who rejected God's commands in the time of Moses, so anyone who despises Christ and His sacrifice can forget about a free ride to heaven.

We noticed earlier in Hebrews how the argument oscillates between high confidence and solemn warning. Both elements occur elsewhere in Scripture, of course, but nowhere are both raised to the intensity that they are in Hebrews, nor do both occur elsewhere in as sharply contrasting a sequence as they do here. This feature of Hebrews adds to its difficulty for commentators: the sermon attracts and repels, mystifies and confuses.

Our study of Hebrews 6:4-6 helps us understand 10:26-31 and the sharp mood swings of the entire book. The two passages stand parallel in thought, with 6:4-6 emphasizing the privileges that come to every Christian and 10:26-31 the certainty of judgment for the despisers of God's grace.

We understand the severity of 10:26-31 in light of the long discussion of 8:1–10:18. This marvelous development highlighted God's gracious provision, His way of salvation. That way led via Calvary, for without blood, there can be no answer to the sin problem. The more wonderful the divine plan, the greater the sin of rejecting that plan.

Some Christians, rightly reasoning that God's love is boundless, have wrongly concluded that everyone eventually must be saved. As much as sentiment might hope that this idea is true, it finds no support in the Bible, and it is ruled out of court by the book of Hebrews. This sermon teaches us that everyone who makes it to heaven will be there only because of the death of Jesus and only because he or she has chosen God's salvation. No one will be there who doesn't want to be there. No one who rejects God's way. No one who mocks Jesus and His cross.

The key word in 10:26-31 is *deliberately* (vs. 26). We will have to battle sin as long as we are in this world, as long as the Spirit has our old nature opposing Him. Victory in this struggle comes from Christ alone—but we must choose Him daily. Just as we first chose Him, confessing Him as Saviour and Lord, so we must decide for Him every day.

As we study the series of exhortations and laminate the argument of Hebrews, we discern a progression of ideas. In 2:1-4 the apostle's concern was with drifting away, neglecting so great a salvation; in 3:6–4:13, with the gradual hardening of the heart through lack of faith; in 5:11–6:19, with lack of growth in Christ and the possibility of falling away from Christ. Here, in 10:26-31, the slide reaches its lowest point, the abyss of open, willful sin, with gross insensitivity to the meaning of Christ's atoning blood.

Is it really possible? Could someone who once rejoiced in the Lord and His Word, who knew the power of the indwelling Spirit and looked forward to the joys of heaven—could such a one conceivably become a castaway from grace, choosing reckless sin instead of Christ?

Yes, says the apostle. Yes, indeed. Within each person lie boundless possibilities—for good or for evil. Renewed and empowered by grace, we may stretch and soar in limitless development and blessing. But if we turn our backs on God, seemingly nothing becomes too despicable for us to commit. The horrors of our twentieth century, with its Hitlers and Idi Amins, have laid bare the terrifying inventiveness of human nature.

We should remember, however, that 10:26-31 is an application. The writer sets out starkly what *might* be, not what has happened. Perhaps Paul saw that some Christians had gone down the slippery slide from 2:1-4 to 10:26-31. Or perhaps he only saw that some might. In any case, he affirmed the congregation: "We are confident of better things in your case" (6:9). But as a faithful steward of the gospel, it was his duty to warn them, and warn them he did!

A Valiant Past

In 10:32-34 we catch a fascinating glimpse of early Christianity. The Hebrew Christians in the past had suffered terribly for their faith. They had been insulted publicly and persecuted and had seen their property confiscated. But throughout this horrendous trial, they had stood their ground for Christ. When they weren't suffering, they took their stand with others who were, including those cast into prison for the name of Jesus.

A refrain of suffering sounds throughout the New Testament. We hear Peter encouraging believers who were persecuted simply for being Christians (1 Pet. 4:12-16), and we catch the thought of sharing in the sufferings of Christ (Phil. 3:10). Most Christians in the West cannot comprehend this aspect of the New Testament; it is altogether outside their experience and passes them by.

But here and there in the West, and more frequently outside the West, in lands where other religions dominate, Christians hear clearly this refrain of suffering. They know public insults, persecution, confiscation of goods, and imprisonment. They know what it means to stand up and be counted as the only Christian in the class, in the school, or in the workplace.

For the first three centuries after Jesus, Christians had no legal rights. The senate had not recognized the new religion, so it remained illicit, and Christians were suspect. They weren't permitted to build buildings for worship (they met in houses), and they could be arrested and tried simply for confessing the name of Christ. Sporadic persecutions broke out, usually regional in nature, depending on the will of the local authorities.

A fascinating letter has come down to us from early in the second century. Pliny, governor of Bithynia, writes to Trajan, emperor of Rome. He tells how he has been dealing with people in the area accused of being Christians and asks his boss's advice:

> My Lord: It is my custom to refer to you everything that I am in doubt about; for who is better able either to correct my hesitation or instruct my ignorance?
>
> I have never been present at trials of Christians; consequently I do not know the precedents regarding the question of punishment or the nature of the inquiry. I have been in no little doubt whether some discrimination is made with regard to age, or whether the young are treated no differently from the older; whether renunciation wins indulgence, or it is of no avail to have abandoned Christianity if one has once been a Christian; whether the very profession of the name is to be punished, or only the criminal practices which go along with the name.
>
> So far this has been my procedure when people were charged before me with being Christians. I have asked the accused themselves if they were Christians; if they said "Yes," I asked them a second and third time, warning them of the penalty; if they persisted I ordered them to be led off to execution. For I had no doubt that, whatever kind of thing it was that they pleaded guilty to, their stubbornness and unyielding obstinacy at any rate deserved to be punished. There were others afflicted with the like madness whom I marked down to be referred to Rome, because they were Roman citizens.
>
> Later, as usually happens, the trouble spread by the very fact that it was being dealt with, and further varieties came to my notice. An anonymous letter was laid before me containing many people's names. Some of these denied that they were Christians or had ever been so; at my dictation they invoked the gods and did reverence with incense and wine to your image, which I had

ordered to be brought for this purpose along with the statues of the gods; they also cursed Christ; and as I am informed that people who are really Christians cannot possibly be made to do any of those things, I considered that the people who did them should be discharged. Others against whom I received information said they were Christians and then denied it; they meant (they said) that they had once been Christians but had given it up: some three years previously, some a longer time, one or two as many as twenty years before. All these likewise both did reverence to your image and the statues of the gods and cursed Christ. . . .

Therefore I deferred further inquiry in order to apply to you for a ruling. The case seemed to me to be a proper one for consultation, particularly because of the number of those who were accused. For many of every age, every class, and of both sexes are being accused and will continue to be accused. Nor has this contagious superstition spread through the cities only, but also through the villages and the countryside. But I think it can be checked and put right. At any rate the temples, which had been well-nigh abandoned, are beginning to be frequented again; and the customary services, which had been neglected for a long time, are beginning to be resumed; fodder for the sacrificial animals, too, is beginning to find a sale again, for hitherto it was difficult to find anyone to buy it. From all this it is easy to judge what a multitude of people can be reclaimed, if an opportunity is granted them to renounce Christianity.

Here it is, just as in 1 Peter 4:12-16—suffering (in this case, dying) for bearing the name Christian.

We also have access to Trajan's reply. The emperor wrote:

My dear Secundus: You have followed the correct procedure in deciding the cases of those who have been charged before you with being Christians. Indeed, no general decision can be made by which a set form of dealing with them could be established. They must not be ferreted out; if they are charged and convicted, they must be punished, provided that anyone who denies that he is a Christian and gives practical proof of that by invoking our gods is to win indulgence by this repudiation, no matter what grounds for suspicion may have existed against him in the past. Anonymous documents which are laid before you should receive no attention in any case; they are a very bad precedent and quite unworthy of the age in which we live (*Epistles of Pliny*, X, 96, 97, quoted in Bruce, *The Spreading Flame*, 169-171).

This correspondence gives us clearer insight into Hebrews 10:32-34. Although Hebrews was probably written some fifty years before Pliny's persecution of Christians, the scenario is almost exactly the same. With such experiences in their past, we can better understand how the Hebrew Christians might be tempted to renounce the faith and join the crowd.

"So," admonishes the apostle, "do not throw away your confidence; it will be richly rewarded" (vs. 35). By perseverance, by continuing in the way of Christ, they would receive the eternal blessings promised by God and made certain by Jesus.

And they had another problem—not merely discouragement from the pressure of a hostile environment, but doubts over the seeming delay in the second coming. Jesus had promised, "I will come back" (John 14:3), and they thought He should have returned long before. As each year dragged by without their seeing Him, the taunts of mockers, the hate, the ridicule, and the injustice seemed harder to bear.

Jesus promised to return, but He didn't say how soon. The Hebrews' problem is our problem. We live more than 1,900 years beyond their generation, and we are still waiting.

The apostle's counsel to them still holds true for us. Jesus is coming! He "will come and will not delay" (vs. 37). God's timetable isn't our timetable. Where we see delay, He sees a perfect plan. "Like the stars in the vast circuit of their appointed path, God's purposes know no haste and no delay" (White, *The Desire of Ages*, 32).

So let us not shrink back. Having come so far, let us hold on and go on. Let us cling to Christ, trusting His promise and never turning back.

For we are pilgrims here, and heaven is our home. The pilgrim lives by faith, not by sight. Translate "those who believe" in verse 39 as "those who have faith," for that is the word (in verb form) that we find here—our old friend *pistis* from 3:6–4:13.

And *pistis*—faith—will structure the long chapter that follows.

■ Getting Into the Word

Hebrews 11

Read Hebrews 11 twice. Note the careful literary construction and the power of the writing. This is one of the great chapters of the Bible, so enjoy it. Can you suggest answers to the following questions?

1. *Faith* **is the key word, but what does it mean? How does it go beyond what we usually call** *belief*?
2. **The King James Version says that "faith is the substance of things hoped for" (1:1). Now look up** *substance* **in an English dictionary, and from the various definitions given, choose the one you think comes closest to what the author of Hebrews meant. Next read Hebrews 11:1 in several other versions of the Bible and notice how each one translates the word** *substance*. **Does this change your conclusion about the author's intended meaning of the word? Write a paragraph explaining which translation you most agree with and why.**
3. **Who is the greatest example of faith in this parade of worthies? Why?**
4. **Classify the deeds of verses 32-38 into some sort of arrangement.**

5. What does *perfect* mean in verse 40?
6. Although the actual word isn't mentioned, look for evidences of a *pilgrimage* theme in this chapter.

■ Exploring the Word

A Title Deed to Heaven—for You and for Me

"Faith," says the apostle, "is being sure of what we hope and certain of what we do not see." These two aspects of faith are not synonymous. The first deals with *time*, the second with *space*. Faith reaches out and grasps the future. Likewise, it lays hold on the world of the unseen—the world that already is but that lies beyond our sight.

Notice how other translations try to convey the thought of Hebrews 11:1.

- "Faith is the *substance* of things hoped for, the *evidence* of things not seen" (King James Version).
- "Faith is the *assurance* of things hoped for, the *conviction* of things not seen" (Revised Standard Version).
- "Faith gives *substance* to our hopes, and makes us *certain* of realities we do not see" (New English Bible).
- "Faith means that we have *full confidence* in the things we hope for, it means being *certain* of things we cannot see" (Phillips, Revised Edition).
- "Only faith can *guarantee* the blessings that we hope for, or *prove* the existence of the realities that at present remain unseen" (Jerusalem Bible).
- "Faith is *confident assurance* concerning what we hope for, and *conviction* about things we do not see" (New American Bible).

For many people today, *faith* suggests a vague religious hope, the believer's crutch, something that belongs to prescientific thinking. But biblical faith—the *pistis* described here and earlier in Hebrews—has a quite different character. The faith of Hebrews 11:1 deals in certainty, not in wish; in fact, not in hope.

The noun translated by "being sure of" in the New International Version is the Greek *hypostasis*. It can mean either "substantial nature, essence, actual being, or reality," or "confidence, conviction, assurance, steadfastness." This word occurs in two other places in Hebrews—first in 1:3, where the Son is called "the stamp of His [God's] *hypostasis*"; and in 3:14, where Paul exhorts Christians to "hold firm the beginning of their *hypostasis*." The contexts of these passages indicate that both uses of the word are being employed. That is, in 1:3 the apostle describes the Son as the stamp of the divine *essence* or *being*, while in 3:14 he tells us to hold firm our *confidence* to the end.

As we look over the various translations of Hebrews 11:1, we see how some versions have opted for the first meaning of *hypostasis* (faith as "substance," as in the King James Version and New English Bible), while others have tilted toward the second (faith as "confidence," "assurance," or "guarantee"). The New International Version belongs in the second group.

The archaeologist's spade has unearthed an understanding of *hypostasis* that sheds light on Hebrews 11:1 Anciently, two parties had disputed ownership of a property (does that sound familiar?). To reinforce her claim before the court, one claimant wrote a letter and sent it with her slave. The slave stopped at an inn for the night—and the inn burned. But the woman's letter was preserved, and also the *hypostasis* that she enclosed with it. And so, after two millennia, the spade uncovered this ancient material. But the *hypostasis* that the woman sent with the letter—what was it?

It was the title deed to the property!

We therefore may accurately translate Hebrews 11:1 to read, "Now faith is the *title deed* to what we hope for, the certainty of what we do not see." Notice how that brings faith's meaning close to our own times!

Let's suppose you've never been to Maui (for most of us, that's probably true). You've heard about that exotic place, and you've always wanted to see it, but you've never been able to get there. One day out of the blue, you get a letter: "Dear _____, as executor of the estate of the late Clarence Goodenough [your Uncle Clary, whom you haven't seen in ages], I have to inform you that he has bequeathed to you his property on Maui. You may obtain the title deed by calling at my office."

With the title deed in hand, the Maui property is yours. Even though you've never seen it, you own it. No doubts, ifs, buts, or maybes—the title deed makes absolutely sure your claim.

That's the apostle's point. Faith, he says, is your title deed and mine to the glorious future God has in store for you. Faith turns hope into reality and the invisible into the concrete.

Thus, faith isn't a one-time matter, a decision to turn from the world and to follow Jesus. Faith is a way of life, an attitude. The man or woman of faith has his or her feet firmly on the ground—*this* is God's world, because He made it and redeemed it. But faith sees beyond the present and beyond this world. The person of faith has dual citizenship. Each is important, and he or she seeks to live in a manner that honors both. Such a stance can come only from outside ourselves. Faith is a gift from God.

Thus, Hebrews 11:1 doesn't give us a definition of *pistis* so much as a description of the way faith works. Certainly the apostle isn't advancing a psychological explanation of faith. Rather, he sets out the two cardinal abilities that faith makes possible—turning hope into reality and the unseen into sight.

Faith's Roll Call

The remainder of the chapter lists men and women of faith—heaven's roll call of those whom God counts great. In panoramic sweep, Paul takes us in order through the Old Testament, from Creation through the antediluvian world, past the sagas of the patriarchs, and on to Moses and the conquest of Canaan.

In measured, stately language the account rolls on, punctuated

over and over with "by faith . . . by faith . . . by faith . . . by faith."
Hebrews 11 rightly stands as one of the greatest chapters of Scripture—magnificent in scope, superb in literary structure, and inspiring for personal Christian living.

The apostle abruptly breaks the sequence with verse 32. His
recitation of the heroes and heroines of faith has brought him as
far as the conquest of Jericho (Joshua 6 in our Bible), but his account is getting long, and he has made his point. With "what more
shall I say?" he wraps up the roll call of faith in a summarizing
paragraph of great power.

As we march with the writer down the columns of the assembled
worthies, we notice that the people chosen provide more than
undifferentiated examples of faith. Throughout the chapter, verse
1, with its two characteristics of *pistis*, looms in the background.
The account is structured to show that everyone mentioned ex-
hibited one or both of faith's hallmarks: They turned hope to reality, and/or they could "see" the invisible.

- verse 3—We grasp Creation only by faith. Faith perceives
  God's ability to form the sensory world out of nothing.
- verse 4—God accepted Abel's sacrifice over his brother's because of Abel's faith. For Cain, the sacrifice was a material
  offering, something to try to please God; for Abel, it was
  more. However dimly, Abel saw beyond the material, the
  concrete, and God commended him for it. Although he is
  dead, "he still speaks"—meaning that those who, like him,
  are people of faith look beyond what is present and catch
  sight of the unseen.
- verse 5—Enoch likewise received God's approval by faith.
  He "pleased" God, which, as the following verse suggests,
  indicates that he "saw" the invisible One and hoped for His
  reward.
- verse 6—This general statement applies to everyone who
  seeks after God. Here we see clearly the twin functions of
  pistis: Faith believes (the verb from the same root as *pistis*)
  that God exists—the conviction of the invisible, and faith

believes that God rewards—the title deed of hope.

- verse 7—Noah "saw" the unseen. He looked to the future also. Faith led him to act, and that action rebuked those around him who were caught up in sensory things.
- verse 8—Abraham's experience demonstrates the two points of Hebrews 11:1. Faith made sure the future inheritance and made "visible" the place of an unknown destination.
- verses 9, 10—After Abraham's arrival in the Promised Land, he continued to live by faith. He had arrived, yet he hadn't arrived. His living in tents showed that existence in Canaan was only temporary, that the *city*—one built by God—was his ultimate goal. He, along with Isaac and Jacob, lived as an heir of God's promise, looking forward. Faith provided him—and them—with the title deed to that city. Faith made it certain.
- verses 11, 12—Abraham and Sarah turned from the sensory world, which afforded no hope of an heir. Faith made the difference. What God promised would come to pass, because it already *was*.
- verses 13-15—This general statement sums up the faith of the patriarchs. We discern clearly the two aspects of faith—the promise, the looking for, the thinking of, the longing for hope; and seeing and welcoming the unseen. This powerful passage describes the life of faith as a pilgrimage, and we shall return to it later for more careful study.
- verses 17-19—Abraham offered up Isaac by faith. The accent here falls on the future: Abraham believed that his son would be resurrected. Back of that assurance of the future, however, was Abraham's confidence in God. Abraham saw the unseen God and trusted that He was able to raise the dead.
- verse 20—When Isaac blessed Jacob and Esau "by faith," he held the future to be guaranteed by God. What God promised would happen. Faith was the title deed.
- verse 21—Jacob's blessing, likewise, looked to the future.
- verse 22—So certain was Joseph that God would keep His

word and bring the Israelites out of Egypt in due time that
he left instructions concerning the disposition of his remains.
Once again, the element of future guarantee is uppermost.

- verse 23—Although this verse does not spell out a specific
  function of faith, the hope (future) aspect seems to be the
  point. Moses' parents disobeyed the king's edict because they
  believed God intended a bright future for their son.
- verses 24-28—This arresting paragraph underscores faith's
  twin elements. On one hand, Moses took the long view over
  the pleasures and treasures of Pharaoh's court. "He was looking ahead to his reward," and faith guaranteed it. But he also
  persevered, fearlessly leading God's people out of Egypt, "because he saw him who is invisible." Likewise, his obedience
  in keeping the Passover and sprinkling blood on the door-
  posts showed his confidence in God—that God would indeed slay Egypt's firstborn son, but that He would protect all
  who acted upon His saving provision.
- verse 29—The Israelites passed through the Red Sea, while
  the Egyptians drowned in it. Faith made the difference. Faith
  set aside the usual order of nature and laid open the invisible
  order, where God dwells and acts.
- verse 30—Likewise, faith brought down the walls of Jericho.
  From the moment God promised Joshua the city would be
  his, it was. By faith, Joshua held the city's title deed in his
  hands.
- verse 31—Even Rahab, an alien and a prostitute, finds a place
  in the gallery of worthies. Although she had in view only a
  short-range future, like those before her, she trusted the word
  of the unseen God.
- verses 32-38—These verses are a summary statement, illustrating the exploits of the great figures out of Israel's past,
  from the fall of Jericho through the rest of the Old Testament. Their deeds fall into three main types: acts of unusual
  political or military greatness ("conquered kingdoms, admin-
  istered justice," "powerful in battle," "routed foreign armies");
  acts outside the normal course of nature ("shut the mouths

of lions, quenched the fury of the flames, and escaped the edge of the sword," "women received back their dead, raised to life again"); and acts of great endurance under insult and extreme suffering ("tortured . . . refused to be released . . . jeers and flogging . . . chained . . . put in prison . . . stoned . . . sawed in two . . . put to death by the sword . . . destitute, persecuted and mistreated . . . wandered in deserts and mountains, and in caves and holes in the ground").

Faith made them different, faith enabled them to do what they did, faith lay behind their extraordinary deeds—this is the point. Because of their faith they became participants in a higher reality, they tapped into divine power, and so their lives and deeds became extraordinary by the canons of human behavior.

So faith leads to *action*. Faith isn't just "belief." Faith motivates and empowers. Faith makes possible the impossible, turns the extraordinary into the ordinary. For faith sees the invisible.

And faith guarantees the future. That is the specific point the apostle makes as he concludes the roll call of faith. None of the giants he has mentioned "received what had been promised" (v. 39). Although some received short-lived fulfillments of their faith—such as Rahab, who was spared the sword—the ultimate reward still awaits God's people. In God's plan, His "something better" will come to all His followers together. Thus, "only together with us" will the heroes and heroines of the ages enter into perfection (vs. 40)—that fullness, finality, and rest of God's eternal home.

And on that note, we can now consider our final concern for this chapter—Christianity as pilgrimage.

Son of the Pilgrim

Earlier in this book, when *pistis* first came to light in 3:7–4:13, we found it associated with rest. And rest, we discovered, involved both the present and the future: We who have *pistis* already enter God's rest, yet rest in its fullness still lies ahead.

These ideas parallel exactly those of Hebrews 11. Whereas in 3:7–4:13 *rest* was the central word and *pistis* less developed, in chapter 11 *pistis* assumes dominant place. *Rest*, in fact, isn't mentioned in chapter 11, but we find equivalents to it in terms like *promise*, *hope*, and *reward*.

The Christian, then, looks beyond this life for his or her final home. Already we experience heavenly realities—we *know* our Lord, who died for us, and He walks with us day by day as our best friend—but the best is yet to be. We live by faith now; one day we shall see Him face to face. One day we shall arrive at that finality—that rest, that perfection or fullness—to which faith is the title deed.

We are pilgrims. Like Abraham, who dwelt in tents and looked forward to the city built by God (vss. 9, 10); like the ill-treated people of God of whom the world was not worthy (vss. 32-38); like the children of faith described in verses 13-16, we are "aliens and strangers on earth."

Many of our hymns reflect a pilgrimage theme. "I'm a pilgrim, and I'm a stranger," "Guide me, O Thou great Jehovah, / Pilgrim through this barren land," "I'm but a stranger here, / Heaven is my home," and so on, we sing. Do we realize what the words are saying?

Christianity as pilgrimage reaches back into the earliest centuries of our faith. Throughout the Middle Ages, devout souls made treks to holy places like Jerusalem and Rome.

Today, however, pilgrimage seems remote from our experience. We know about the "pilgrims" who came to North America on the *Mayflower* and perchance have read John Bunyan's classic *Pilgrim's Progress*. The Moslems, we know, still take pilgrimage seriously. The *hajj* (visit to Mecca) stands as a lifelong goal for every adherent. But what does "pilgrimage" have to say to us who believe in Jesus, who live in homes, not tents; who drive automobiles, and don't walk?

A great deal, actually. Hebrews 11, and especially verses 13-16, where the pilgrim motif comes into sharp focus, speaks powerfully to Christians living today—if we are willing to listen as God speaks His word to us.

When we study pilgrimage in general, we find four features: separation, journeying to a predetermined place, religious purpose, and accompanying hardship. We find all these elements in Abraham's experience—leaving Ur, journeying to the Promised Land, remaining a covenant keeper, who will become father of the faithful, and encountering difficulties. Hebrews 11:13-16, likewise, shows these characteristics. The "aliens and strangers" have *left* a country, and they are on the move, looking for a better country—a heavenly one. Though the way is long, and they suffer pain, they know that God claims them as His own even now, and one day they will see Him face to face.

Often you hear people speak of pilgrimage in a nonreligious sense, as when they refer to the course of their life, their journey. But Christianity as pilgrimage means much more. It means we have chosen to *leave behind* a way of life that most others find attractive. It means that we don't merely *go* through life, but that we are journeying toward a *goal*. It means that this life isn't the end for us, but merely a prelude to something better in God's eternal home. And it means that the hardship that comes to us is more than "the university of hard knocks"—it is permitted and used by a loving Lord, who will turn it for our good. It means that we can trust God, even in the hardest times.

In light of the overall plan of Hebrews, we see how effectively the exhortation of 10:19–11:40, and especially the entire eleventh chapter, fits the apostle's purposes. The heavenly sanctuary, with Jesus as our great High Priest, and His all-sufficient sacrifice— this rests upon our ability to "see" the unseen. The real is not the Jerusalem temple, but the heavenly; not earthly priests, but Jesus; not lambs, goats, and bulls, but Jesus' blood that makes atonement.

And in the midst of a society that rejects Jesus, surrounded by pressures to renounce Him and go back to the pagan crowd, only the life of *faith* can stay unbowed. Faith guarantees the future and sees the invisible. Thus faith enables the Christian to endure. Faith brings faith*fulness*—no shrinking back, no drifting away, no gradual hardening of the spiritual arteries, no sluggishness or torpor. Only a clear-eyed looking to Jesus and running with unbroken stride the race set before us.

The final two chapters will carry on these themes and apply them further as the apostle concludes his sermon.

■ Applying the Word

1. How can I encourage those I associate with every day to be more loving and live a life of good deeds?

2. What spiritual benefits do I gain from worshiping with other Christians in church that I could never gain from watching the same worship service on my television screen at home? Why is it especially important that I maintain regular church attendance as the second coming of Christ draws near?

3. How can I look forward to the coming time of trouble without fear? Which is a better preparation for that time—cultivating a relationship with Jesus or Christian character development? What reason can I give for my answer?

4. How can I be sure that I will never turn my back on Christ and give up my Christian faith?

5. What issues in my life right now are stretching my faith the most? Which account of faith in Hebrews 11 is especially helpful in dealing with these issues? Why?

6. Abraham believed in a city "whose architect and builder is God" (vs. 10). Four thousand years later, Christians are still looking for that city. How can I be sure that my faith in the nearness of Christ's return is not just religious extremism?

7. What rewards has God placed in my life that strengthen my faith? What rewards do I receive because I believe, and what rewards does God give everyone, regardless of their belief (see Matt. 5:44, 45)?

8. What does it mean today to live the life of a Christian

pilgrim as described in Hebrews 11? How is the life of a pilgrim different from life the way the world lives it? How is it different from what we usually think of as the "normal" Christian life?

■ Researching the Word

1. Use a concordance to look up all the occurrences of *Abraham* in the New Testament, and make a note of everything the New Testament says about Abraham's faith. Compare this with the actual story of Abraham as recorded in Genesis 12-22, including the incidents recorded in Genesis 15. Then answer these questions:
   a. How perfect does my faith have to be in order for it to be acceptable to God?
   b. What was it about Abraham's life that God found acceptable as a life of faith in spite of his flaws? What is He looking for in my life as acceptable faith in spite of my flaws?
   c. How can I expect God to relate to me when my imperfect faith causes me to do things that seem to show a lack of faith?
2. With the help of a concordance, study the way *faith* (including the words *belief* and *believe*) is used in the synoptic Gospels (Matthew, Mark, and Luke), Romans, Galatians, and James. Compare your findings with the presentation of faith in Hebrews 11. What conclusion do you reach as to the essential meaning of the wrong *faith* (*pistis*)?
3. Study the Jews' rejection of Jesus in the Gospel of John. What similarities do you find between these stories and the consequences of rejecting the truth that Paul describes in Hebrews 6:4-6 and 10:26-31? What do you learn from John's Gospel that can help you to avoid the terrible consequences described in Hebrews?

∎ Further Study of the Word

1. For a study of Christianity as pilgrimage, see W. G. Johnsson, *In Absolute Confidence*, 150-160.
2. For a discussion of the meaning of faith in Hebrews, see P. E. Hughes, *A Commentary on the Epistle to the Hebrews*, 437-443.
3. For a verse-by-verse treatment of Hebrews 10:19–11:40, see F. F. Bruce, *The Epistle to the Hebrews*, rev. ed., 248-331.

CHAPTER NINE

The Better City

Hebrews 12:1–13:25

The apostle has reached the concluding part of his sermon. Behind us is the masterly presentation of Jesus as High Priest and sacrifice and the glorious parade of the "greats" of faith. His final remarks, covering Hebrews 12 and 13 in our Bible, will wrap up and tie off the lessons for life that he wishes his hearers to take away.

One can too readily pass over these chapters lightly, viewing them as a mere addendum to the powerful arguments and resounding literary constructions of the first eleven chapters. That would be a mistake. However today's commentators may treat these chapters, they were vital to the author. They are filled with practical concerns, because his concerns for the reader are practical. Hebrews is a sermon, meant to lead the people to a change of life.

So we find here the chief counsels of the book once more. Those motivations to carry on in the Christian way without flagging—they come as before with positive suggestions and also in terms of warning. The ideas are the same as we have encountered earlier, but we do not have mere repetition—the apostle is too skilled and creative a communicator for that. Rather, we find the earlier practical concerns couched in new settings, with several fresh metaphors of brilliant power.

Thus, in chapter 12 we meet, in turn, exhortations to faithful endurance (verses 1-13), a reminder of the privileges of belonging to the worship of heaven with Jesus as our High Priest (14-24), and warnings (25-29). Chapter 13 gathers together sundry advice (vss. 1-19) and concludes with a benediction and personal greetings.

215

■ Getting Into the Word

Hebrews 12:1-29

Read Hebrews 12 twice. Reflect on the ideas that you en-counter and where you found them earlier in the sermon. After thoughtful, prayer reflection on these chapters, con-sider the following questions.

1. List the ways in which the Christian life is like a race. In what ways is it unlike a modern contest?
2. Does God call us to do just what Jesus did, or does He invite us to trust what Jesus did for us?
3. Which passage in chapter 12 repeats the severe warnings of 6:4-6 and 10:26-31? Where is the emphasis placed in this passage?
4. Consider the problem of human suffering in light of the instruction in 12:4-11.
5. Make a list of the contrasts between the description of Mount Sinai in 12:18-21 with Mount Zion in verses 22-24. Why does the portrayal of Sinai seem so negative here?
6. How can Paul say, "You have come to Mount Zion, to the heavenly Jerusalem," when he called God's people "aliens and strangers on earth" in 11:13 and will say in 13:14—"For here we do not have an enduring city"? Does our study of the meaning of faith from the last chapter help resolve the dilemma?
7. When will God shake the earth and the heavens (12:26)? Locate other passages of Scripture that speak about this shaking.

■ Exploring the Word

The long line of worthies marches unbroken through chapter 11, but with the opening words of the new chapter, the spotlight falls squarely on the Hebrews themselves: "Therefore, since *we* . . . let us." As the men and women of old lived by faith, so the followers of Christ must press onward, enduring without wavering, certain that they are children of a loving Father.

Running Life's Race

The scene comes straight out of a sports meet. Spectators pack the stands to watch the athletes vie for the gold. Down on the field, the runners are stretching and psyching themselves up for the moment when the starting gun will launch them into furious contest. Two thousand years haven't diminished the energy and excitement of Hebrews 12:1, 2.

Yet we find differences. Athletes in the ancient olympiads trained with weights strapped to their bodies. On the day of the race, they would take these weights off (in fact, they competed in the nude), and their bodies would feel as light as a feather. That is the background of Paul's advice, "Let us throw off everything that hinders" in 12:1—or, as the King James Version has it, "Let us lay aside every weight."

More important, in Paul's time, as in ours, only one runner could win the prize. But in the race of life, everyone who completes the course is a winner. As Christians, we do not compete against one another. Rather, we help one another to the finish line. If anything, we compete with ourselves, striving by God's grace to reach the highest level of performance of which we are capable.

The spectators—the "witnesses" of 12:1—are probably the heroes of chapter 11. Not that they have gone to heaven and are now looking down on us, because 11:39 tells us they haven't yet received the promise. But the silent testimony of their faithful lives serves as an example to us. We all have one life to live, one chance for greatness, one opportunity to develop every excellency and to improve every talent. They had their day in the sun, and they ran well; now we have ours.

And Jesus—He is there. He stands at the tape, His eyes following our progress, His voice cheering us on. He Himself ran the course and finished victoriously. Now, He helps us in our race. Thus He is not only faith's author but its perfecter. We begin with Him and end with Him. Our salvation is all of Him and of Him only.

We can never do what He has done. He comes to us in these days and calls us, as He called of old to the fishermen by the lake, "Follow Me!" He calls us to be disciples, to walk in His steps, to carry on the work of healing, teaching, and preaching that He began. So we come after Him, tracing the course of life that He ran.

But we can never do just what He did. Between Him and us, a qualitative gap will and must ever exist. He is our Saviour, our High Priest. We are the worshipers. He is the Sacrifice; we are sinners in need of help.

Verse 2 presents an interesting alternative in translation: "*For the joy set before him*" comes from the Greek preposition *anti*, which has a similar meaning to its English counterpart. Thus, we can understand the apostle to mean, not that Jesus endured the cross and the shame because He looked beyond and saw the joy that would follow after, but that *instead of* the joys of heaven, He came to earth to suffer and die, to be mocked, scorned, and rejected by the very ones He came to save.

I favor this alternative translation. I think it fits best with, and echoes, the earlier portrayals of Jesus' humanity in Hebrews—the accent on Jesus' suffering in 2:9, 10 and the vivid description of Gethsemane in 5:7, 8. In neither of the descriptions does the apostle suggest that Jesus was sustained in His trials by the hope of what lay beyond His death. To the contrary, we find only a graphic account of the reality of His experiences.

However we choose to translate *anti* in 12:2, the main point of the passage shines bright: "Let us fix our eyes on Jesus." We heard this call early in the sermon—"Fix your thoughts on Jesus" (3:1). Now it comes again. Like bookends, this invitation and challenge frames the counsel of Hebrews.

Fix your thoughts—not on others, even though they may be worthy examples of faithfulness. Not on the past. Not on yourself. Only on Jesus.

The 1954 British Empire Games, held in Vancouver, British Columbia, provide a remarkable illustration of Hebrews 12:1, 2. The mile race that was held there is considered to be one of the greatest races—perhaps the greatest race—of all time. It pitted the two fastest men in the world over one mile—Roger Bannister and John Landy.

Following his usual approach, Landy started fast. Unlike most runners, Landy's method was to move to the head of the pack early and by the sheer power of his physique outlast the other runners, who would reserve strength for a final thrust at the tape. The race was clearly between Bannister and Landy. Soon the other runners were dropping back, leaving Landy out in front, with Bannister well behind him.

At the end of each quarter mile, the times were announced, and with each declaration, the stands rocked. Landy and Bannister were setting a blazing pace, one that would surely set a new world record. But who would get to the tape first?

So the runners came to the final lap, the final quarter mile. Landy was in front, ahead of Bannister, as he had been throughout the race. Ahead of him stretched the tape, looming closer and closer. Somewhere behind him was Bannister. And then a deafening roar arose in the stands. Landy knew what it meant: Bannister was making his last desperate effort to catch Landy! The tape was getting closer and closer and the roar louder and louder. Landy knew that Bannister in his last great effort was catching up. But where was he?

Just before the tape, Landy turned his head so he could see just where Bannister was. And Bannister, seizing the psychological moment, threw himself past Landy on the other side and just beat him to the tape!

A statue in Vancouver memorializes the moment. It shows one runner breasting the tape while the other, just a tad behind him, turns his head. What a portrayal of the lesson of Hebrews 12:1, 2—"Let us fix our eyes on Jesus"!

The remainder of this exhortation to faithfulness, verses 4-13, places the Hebrews in the context of children being disciplined by a loving heavenly Father. The passage supplies strong hints that the readers already are suffering for their faith. We read, "Endure hardship as discipline (vs. 7), and, "No discipline seems pleasant at the time, but painful" (vs. 11). Verse 4, with its reference to suffering "to the point of shedding your blood," implies that the hardships that lie ahead may even bring death to the followers of Jesus.

They shouldn't be surprised by suffering, but rather should expect it—that is the point that runs through the discussion. The Old Testament text, Proverbs 3:11, 12, conveys this idea and shapes the presentation. So hardship and suffering in the hands of a loving Father can be turned into a positive function. They show that God takes an interest in us—that we are His children, not illegitimate—and God uses trials for our good, producing a "harvest of righteousness and peace" (vs. 11).

The word translated as "discipline" in verses 5-11 is the Greek *paideia*, which lies behind our English terms for education, such as *pedagogy*. *Discipline* accurately reflects the meaning of the Greek, if we understand discipline as training and not necessarily as something negative. Unfortunately, discipline has dropped out of favor in our times because it has come to be associated with harshness—the marine corps drill sergeant pushing soldiers in boot camp to the physical and psychological limit. We still see the positive sense of the word, however, in the academic arena, as scholars refer to their field of expertise as their "discipline."

Christians need to recover the biblical idea of discipline. No, we don't need the old "spare the rod and spoil the child" line, which too often becomes abusive as the big guy vents his anger against the little one. What we need to find again is that sense of training ourselves, of growth into maturity and depth, of concentration on the task, the setting aside of immediate gratification that biblical discipline connotes.

We should note that this passage doesn't provide an answer to one of the greatest questions of our age and of every age—suffering. Why do bad things happen to good people? Why do bad people seem to have it so good? Why did God let six million Jews die in the death camps? This question has made atheists of countless Jews and led millions of non-Jews to doubt. We see the images thrown onto our television screens each night—emaciated children in African countries, genocidal killing in the Balkans, violence in the streets of our cities—and we wonder why God doesn't do something about it.

No, we don't find a theodicy here—a reasoned explanation that seeks to defend God. But we do find a *religious* answer, one that touches us in our own pain. The picture we get of God is a kind, loving Father who tenderly watches over all that comes our way. He isn't the author of evil; suffering comes from another source. But God can take even evil and turn it to a good purpose—if we let him. Out of suffering He can produce lives of beauty, peace, and trust.

Suffering never leaves us untouched. We either draw closer to the Teacher, or we pull away, embittered. We become a John Bunyan, a Helen Keller—or an atheist.

O What a Beautiful City

Hebrews 12:14-24 reminds us of our great privileges. We are pilgrims, on our way to a glorious future in God's presence, but already we have much in which to rejoice. Salvation isn't only ahead of us; it is here now!

The three paragraphs of this section develop two lines of reasoning. In the first, verses 14-17, we learn about our privileges from a negative example. Esau was a spiritual klutz—he simply didn't value what really counted. He traded his birthright for a bowl of beans. Talk about faith as something that hopes in God and looks to the future—Esau lived in a different world! His life was the here and now; to fill his belly meant more to him than some nebulous blessing of the firstborn.

So the warning comes through loud and clear to the Hebrew Christians—and to us. Remember salvation so great. Remember Jesus. Remember what God has in store for you. And so—keep your priorities in order!

The apostle's treatment of Esau reminds us of his strong words in 6:4-6 and 10:26-31. In all three passages, we find the loss of something precious and the grim thought that it may be gone forever. "It is impossible" (6:4), "no sacrifice for sins is left" (10:26), we heard earlier. Now we hear, "He was rejected. He could bring about no change of mind, though he sought the blessing with tears" (vs. 17).

We find the same thrust in each of these passages. Although 12:16, 17 is the shortest of the three, its thought is identical with the two earlier treatments. Whereas 6:4-6 focused on the high privileges that have come with Jesus' salvation and 10:26-31 on the certainty of judgment if we despise His saving death, 12:16, 17 highlights the certainty of loss of God's spiritual blessings if we do not value them.

In contrast to the doleful example of Esau, the next two paragraphs give a brilliant summary of the blessings Jesus has brought. But the apostle doesn't merely reiterate the points he has made earlier; he gathers them together in an illustration of great power and beauty. Access, confidence, blood, covenant, superiority—these marvelous ideas that we saw developed in detail through the first ten chapters rise up again but are now tied together under the motif of the better city, the new Jerusalem.

The predominant thought from the two paragraphs, which stand in juxtaposition, is the full, unhindered access to God that Jesus has brought. Paul picks up the story of the giving of the law in Exodus 19, 20 and underscores its terrifying aspects—the darkness, gloom, and fire; the words that pierced the hearts of the Israelites with fear; the trumpet blast; and especially the prohibition against touching the sacred mountain (even an animal that strayed up to it had to be stoned). Moses himself trembled with fear.

This portrayal of Sinai, while drawn from the Old Testament, is sharply different from many of our presentations. We tend to focus on the majesty and grandeur of the event as the Lord Himself uttered the moral law, the foundation and basis for every individual and every society.

Both pictures of Sinai are accurate; both come from the same account. What we find in Hebrews is a retelling of that grand event that conforms with the pattern of comparing and contrasting the old and the new that runs through the entire sermon. We found the formula in the opening paragraph of Hebrews, and we see it again here: The old isn't bad—after all, it came from God—but the new is better. So at Sinai, God was behind the terrifying sights and sounds (although He is referred to only obliquely in the "voice speaking words"); but at Mount Zion, the heavenly Jerusalem, God *welcomes* His people.

The description of the better city leaps and sings with holy joy. Myriads of angels share the worship of heaven with men and women redeemed from a sinful planet; they fellowship together as servants of the King of love. And these people from earth— they do not sit in a corner or way up in the balcony in the seats with a restricted view; no, they have been "made perfect," made whole again by the glorious salvation God has provided. (Thus, we find the dominant access theme coupled with the perfecting/ cleansing benefit as shown in 8:1–10:18.)

And at the center of this panoply of praise stands Jesus! He is the mediator of the new covenant, who brings forgiveness of sins and cleansing of defilement. His sprinkled blood has power to do what multiplied millions of animal sacrifices could never accomplish for us. In the center is where Jesus belongs, because by Him and in Him alone we have a right to the celebration of the heavenly city.

His blood speaks! It speaks "a better word"! A word of hope. A word of comfort. A word of cleansing. A word of power. A word of welcome.

The law speaks from Sinai, and that word terrifies us. The law condemns us, excludes us. The law—holy, just, and good—sets out God's standard, God's requirement. That mark is so far beyond our possibilities that we can only wonder at it and turn away in disappointment. For that work speaks God's judgment on our lostness, our alienation, our failure, our defilement.

But through Jesus' blood we hear a better word. "Welcome home, children; you *belong* here! Welcome to the heavenly Jerusalem. Welcome to the city that God's people, strangers and pilgrims on the earth, have sought through the centuries. Welcome to the angel choir. Welcome to joy unutterable and endless delights. Welcome in the name of Jesus—welcome through the blood of Jesus!"

Hebrews 12:18-24 presents one of the most moving and brilliant passages in all of Scripture. Yet rarely does one hear mention of it; rarely do preachers attempt to expound it. Perhaps its neglect stems from its seeming obscurity and difficulty. And difficult, indeed, it is—if one tries to understand it in isolation from the rest of the book. But when the reader begins where the author began, in 1:1, and works forward through Hebrews, he or she finds here familiar ideas. They are the chief theological themes of the entire sermon, gathered together in one final construction of great power and beauty.

One question from 12:18-24 still confronts us, however. How can the apostle tell the readers that they already *have come* to the heavenly Jerusalem, that they *have come* to the joyful assembly of angels? In the same way that throughout the sermon he can say: "We *have* a great high priest" (4:14); "let us . . . *approach* the throne of grace with confidence" (4:16); "we do *have* such a high priest" (8:1); "we *have* confidence to enter the [sanctuary]" (10:19); and "let us *draw near* to God . . . in full assurance" (10:22).

The key to his thinking is the great idea from chapter 11—faith. Faith sees the invisible; faith lays hold of the unseen; faith guarantees the future. Jesus is real; so is the heavenly temple, where He ministers; so is the heavenly Jerusalem. By faith we enter that temple, approaching the presence of the King of the universe. And by faith we participate already in the worship of the holy city, for faith assures our future.

Notice how faith turns on its head our customary scale of reality. The evidence of our senses tells us that a mountain in Arabia that we can see and touch is the real; but faith says No! The real lies beyond our sight, hearing, touch; the real is Mount Zion.

A Final Warning

As 12:18-24 gives the final summary of the benefits of the salvation provided by Jesus, so 12:25-29 sounds, for a last time, the warnings of Hebrews.

How quickly the pendulum swings in this book of rapid changes! No place for fear and doubt, for the sermon rings with confidence and assurance based, not on ourselves, but on Jesus' person and work; but no place for sitting on our hands either. The gospel comes as promise—promise to be made concrete through the life of faith.

So the present possession of salvation comes tempered with the caution that we may lose it. God will not fail. His "kingdom . . . cannot be shaken" (vs. 28), but we may fail Him and lose our place in it.

As before, the warning is shaped on the logic of lesser-greater. Those who refused him who warned them on earth (that is, Moses) did not escape, so those who refuse the One who warns us from heaven (that is, God) will have even less chance to escape. The reasoning is exactly parallel in form and content to 2:1-4 and 10:26-31.

However, we find an additional element in this warning. Whereas the apostle in the other passages argued on the basis of the "salvation so great" provided by Jesus, here, he includes an eschatological factor. He builds on his description of Mount Sinai in 12:18-21, adding, "At that time his [God's] voice shook the earth" (a reference to Exodus 19:18—"the whole mountain trembled violently"). Then he compares and contrasts this with the prediction of a far greater earthquake in Haggai 2:6, in which not only the earth but also the heavens will be shaken.

So we find a double set of contrasts: God greater than Moses and the universal shaking instead of the earthquake on Mount Sinai. God, who provides salvation fully and freely in His Son Jesus Christ comes as Judge of all the earth. He will separate the permanent from the temporary; and His testing of everything both in heaven and earth will screen out those who are faithful from those who are unfaithful.

Let us therefore heed His warning, lest we, too, fall under divine judgment!

■ Getting Into the Word

Hebrews 13:1-25

Read through Hebrews 13 twice, then attempt to answer the following study questions:

1. This chapter reveals a good deal about the situation and problems of the Hebrew Christians. List all that you learn here about their spiritual needs.
2. Reflect on the list you have just drawn up. Which of these needs or problems do you find among Christians today?
3. Use a concordance to look up the phrase *outside the camp* (vss. 11, 13) in the Old Testament. What sort of people or activities would be found "outside the camp"?
4. Is Hebrews ultimately a call to God's people to *separate from* society or to bring the news of Jesus' salvation *to all* society?
5. Explain 13:14—"We are looking for a city," in light of what you read in 12:22—"You *have come* to . . . the heavenly Jerusalem."
6. Compare the closing benediction in Hebrews (13:20, 21) with other apostolic benedictions (Rom. 15:13; 16:25-27; 1 Cor. 16:23; 2 Cor. 13:14; 2 Pet. 3:18; Jude 24, 25; Rev. 22:20, 21).

■ Exploring the Word

Hebrews 13 falls into two parts: sundry counsels for Christian living that show how the gospel impacts the gamut of existence (1-19) and the apostolic benediction and closing remarks (20-25).

A "Shopping List" for Christians—in Any Age

The sundry advice of 13:1-19 is diverse and follows no particular order. Among other things, it takes in relations among Christians, attitudes to others, marriage, economic matters, and the place of leaders:

1. *Love each other as brothers.* Paul can write, "*Keep on* loving each other," rather than, "*Love* each other." So we see a warm, caring Christian community (vs. 1).
2. *Keep on entertaining strangers also.* Love extends outside the church family circle to take in the wayfarer (vs. 2).
3. *Show compassion toward others, in prison and suffering.* We see here a picture of Christians who were undergoing persecution, as the Hebrews once had endured (10:32-34). While the congregation or congregations addressed here were presently free of trouble, they were to identify with their suffering brothers and sisters (vs. 3).
4. *Maintain purity in marriage and sexual relations.* Adultery and sexual immorality were problems then as now (vs. 4).
5. *Avoid love of money and materialism.* Instead of placing confidence in transitory riches, the Hebrews should trust in the unfailing God (vss. 5, 6).
6. *Follow the example of godly leaders* (vs. 7).
7. *Beware of strange teachings.* The apostle does not elaborate as to their nature. Possibly they concern ceremonial foods, which are his next thought, or he may refer to undue veneration of angels and speculations about Melchizedek (vs. 9). (See our earlier treatment of Hebrews 1:5-14 and chapter 7.)
8. *Follow the footsteps of Jesus,* which lead "outside the camp," bearing the same disgrace. These verses (11-13) call for additional comment later.
9. Although Jesus alone is the true Priest, *all we who believe in Him are now priests* in the sense that we have access to God. The "sacrifices" we offer are praise to Christ and good works to others (vss. 15, 16).

10. *Submit to the authority of faithful church leaders* (vs. 17).
11. *Pray.* Pray for the apostles; pray that the writer may be restored to them soon (vss. 18, 19).

As we look over this list, two aspects from it impress us. First, how wide ranging it is. The salvation that Jesus brings changes us into new people. The gospel impacts every aspect of our living—from our beds to our pocketbooks, from our beliefs to our attitudes. In particular, it transforms relationships to fellow church members, to leaders, and to strangers. Christianity means much more than a belief system—it is a new way of life.

Second, we notice how contemporary the counsel sounds. We can go down the eleven-point list above and check off every item as something important for life in our own times. With all the changes the industrial and information revolutions have brought us, with all our knowledge and technology, we are still human. We have the same needs personally, socially, spiritually; we face the same allurements to evil and to worldliness. Though the congregation of Hebrews is separated from us by a vast gulf of time and culture, it seems surprisingly like a church in North America today.

And so God's Word speaks to us. It reminds us who we are—sons and daughters of the King of heaven, bought by the blood of Jesus. It lifts our sights up and away from the secular and the material; it beckons us out of the petty, self-centered circle that we draw around ourselves. It calls us to a life utterly different from those who do not know or follow our Lord. It calls us to live by faith—in Jesus.

For *there* He is, right in the center of the list, in the center, where He belongs. "Jesus Christ is the same yesterday and today and forever" (vs. 8). He is the One who left heaven to live among us and to die as a sinless Sacrifice for us. He is our great High Priest in heaven above. And He is the One who will come back soon for His people.

Jesus Christ—our unchanging Saviour, Lord, and Friend!

For the last time, the apostle returns to the language of temples, priests, and sacrifices (vss. 10-15). Now, however, he doesn't have any theological point to establish; rather, he uses this familiar setting to drive home a couple of practical concerns.

First, he encourages the Hebrew Christians that they need not feel excluded from the Jewish system. For believers in Jesus out of a Jewish background, the hostility they experienced from those of their own race must have been painful, and they would have felt keenly the loss of participation in the services of the temple. For some years, Jewish Christians continued to worship in the temple, but gradually they found themselves no longer welcome. Paul on his last visit to Jerusalem became the target of a riot because of misunderstandings when he attempted to follow the temple services (Acts 21:17-36).

To any reader feeling disenfranchised from the temple, the apostle writes, "We have an altar from which those who minister at the tabernacle have no right to eat" (13:10). Rather than feeling cut off, they should feel privileged. That temple far surpasses the structure on earth.

He next draws a homiletical lesson from the sin offerings of the old system (vss. 11-13). When the blood was brought into the sanctuary (sometimes an alternative procedure was followed, as the priests ate a portion of the offering within the sanctuary; see, for example, Lev. 6:24-30), the bodies of the animals were burned outside the camp. In like manner, suggests Paul, Jesus suffered and died "outside the camp."

The term *outside the camp* occurs several times in the Old Testament in connection with the wandering tribes in the desert. It suggests an unclean place, a place of separation and death, where lepers roamed, criminals were executed, and the bodies of animals used for sin offerings were burned (Lev. 13:46; 24:14; Duet. 23:14).

And that is where Jesus died! Not in the temple, not in the place consecrated for sacrifices, not even within the precincts of the holy city. But "outside the city gate" on profane ground, at the unclean place where criminals were executed and lepers roamed and animals' bodies were burned.

O the wonder of God's plan for our redemption! Look at our Priest—Jesus. No colorful robes for Him, no schooling in rabbinical lore, and no pedigree to enable Him to even make the claim of priest. Our Priest has no parentage, patron, or possessions, no human sponsor, only Himself.

And look at His sacrifice! Dragged through a kangaroo court, the object of mocking and humiliation, forsaken even by His miserable band of followers, He died on a felon's cross, executed by the Romans. But He was God's offering for the sins of the world, Himself the Priest, Himself the Sacrifice.

And where is His temple? We can point to no golden edifice on Mount Zion, no cathedral or palace. He was born in a manger; He never had a temple. But His sanctuary is the real, the genuine, of which earthly temples were but faint copies.

So, says the apostle, let us join Him "outside the camp." We don't *need* to be part of the earthly temple now; we belong with Him. Therein lie profound implications for Christian living. Because Jesus died in a profane place, He has removed all separations of temples and holy places on this earth. His cross has sanctified every "outside the camp"—every secular spot. He has claimed this whole world for Himself by pitching His cross outside the camp. We no longer live in a two-compartment world of sacred and profane; all is Christ's, and our every act is to be for Christ.

And so verses 15 and 16—the world is holy, and so we all are priests, offering sacrifices of praise and good works.

Once more, for the last time, the apostle refers to "the city" (vs. 14). But unlike 12:22, where he could say that Christians already "have come to Mount Zion, to the heavenly Jerusalem," here, he states that "we are looking for the city that is to come." How can this be—we have arrived, but we haven't arrived?

Because Christians live in the tension of the "already" and the "not yet." *Already* we belong to Jesus, *already* He has saved us, *already* He has opened the door to the heavenly sanctuary for us, *already* He has cleansed us from our defilement. But we are strangers and pilgrims still, on the way to our final home: have we arrived, *not yet* do we see the city, *not yet* do we see the temple, *not yet* do we see Jesus—only by faith, *not yet.*

The city is like God's rest (3:7–4:13). That rest is already present, and the Sabbath is an illustration of it, but rest in its fullness still lies ahead.

In fact, the entire New Testament displays the same tension of already/not yet. We find it as early as Jesus' sayings about "the kingdom," where some texts refer to the present and others to the future (e.g., Matt. 5:3; 6:10; 25:34; Luke 17:21).

Blessing and Farewell

The apostolic benediction (vss. 20, 21) seems especially appropriate to the sermon. Its first half echoes the theology of the document by the reference to "the blood of the eternal covenant," while the remainder points to the outworking of this theology in the lives of the readers.

This blessing, stately in form, majestic in language, and fundamental in conception, speaks powerfully to us in these times. But we wonder—did this benediction arise from the author's own mind as he was impressed by the Holy Spirit, or does he here call into service a blessing already in use among Christians?

Inasmuch as we find no other occurrence of the blessing among the early Christian writings, we cannot settle the question with certainty. I incline toward the latter possibility, however. While the one who wrote the whole marvelous sermon certainly was capable of framing 13:20, 21, I wonder why he would introduce two ideas at this late point—the resurrection of Christ and the shepherd/sheep motif. Neither of these ideas occur elsewhere in Hebrews, although they are common in other New Testament writings. I suspect the apostle either quoted an existing benediction or drew upon liturgical language in common use among the early Christians.

Only in the closing verses (vss. 23-25) do we find the personal marks characteristic of a New Testament epistle. They do not, however, change our conception of the work as a whole—it is a "word of exhortation," a sermon.

And what a sermon! How I would love to have heard it delivered in person! And how I would like to hear its ideas sounding from pulpits across the land today!

My hope and my prayer is that this study of Hebrews, as inadequate as it is to capture and unlock the glories of this book, may in its own way be used of God to spark a renewed interest in the sermon. Whether or not preachers take up the messages of Hebrews, so faith building, so up-to-date—every one of us has access to them—we have the sermon; we have the Bible. May we each hear the word of the Lord.

Today, if you hear his voice,
do not harden your hearts.

■ Applying the Word

Hebrews 12:1–13:25

1. What trials am I experiencing at this time? What part of Paul's advice in 12:2-11 seems especially relevant in helping me through them?
2. Why did Esau give up his birthright (see Genesis 25:19-34)? What issues in his life at that time are present in my life today? Why did he not receive the blessing, even though he sought it with tears? How can I be assured of God's blessing when I seek it?
3. In 12:22-24 is a list of several places to which the apostle says that I have "come." What does each of these "places" mean to me in my spiritual life?
4. In 12:29 Paul says that "our God is a consuming fire." Is that good news or bad news for me? Do I feel fear when I read those words, or do I feel confidence and joy? Why? How did Paul intend that I should respond?
5. As I review Paul's bits and pieces of advice in 13:1-19, which ones seem most applicable to my life right now?
6. How has God equipped me for doing His will, as He promised in 13:20, 21?

■ Researching the Word

1. With the help of a concordance, look up all the references to *kingdom* in the four Gospels. Classify each one as "already" or "not yet." What unique contribution does each slant make to your spiritual life?
2. Scan through the various forms of the word *shake* in your concordance, and look up those that seem especially relevant to Paul's use of the word in Hebrews 12:26, 27. Is Paul talking in generalities, or does he have something specific in mind? What other Bible texts might help answer this question? Whatever your conclusion, of what spiritual value can it be in your life right now?
3. Make a list of Bible characters you can think of who endured trials. Look them up, and read them, and after each one, go back and read Hebrews 12:2-11. Ask yourself how closely each one came to "following" Paul's advice and what lessons you can gain from each one for your own life.

■ Further Study of the Word

1. For a verse-by-verse commentary on Hebrews 12:1–13:25, see F. F. Bruce, *The Epistle to the Hebrews*, rev. ed., 332-392.
2. For a commentary with heavy reference to the Greek text, see B. F. Westcott, *The Epistle to the Hebrews*, 391-452.